T0193207

April's Revolution

April's Revolution

A MODERN PERSPECTIVE OF AMERICAN MEDICAL CARE OF CIVIL WAR SOLDIERS AND AFRICAN SLAVES

PAULETTE SNOBY, RN, BSN, MPA

iUniverse LLC
Bloomington

APRIL'S REVOLUTION
A Modern Perspective of American Medical Care
of Civil War Soldiers and African Slaves

iUniverse books may be ordered through booksellers or by contacting:

iUniverse LLC
1663 Liberty Drive
Bloomington, IN 47403
www.iuniverse.com
1-800-Authors (1-800-288-4677)

ISBN: 978-1-4917-2683-9 (sc)
ISBN: 978-1-4917-2682-2 (hc)
ISBN: 978-1-4917-2681-5 (e)

Library of Congress Control Number: 2014903706

Printed in the United States of America.

iUniverse rev. date: 03/06/2014

Contents

APPRECIATION

As I began this journey, my mentor, Wiley Sword, provided sound advice and the opportunity to examine his amazing collection of authentic Civil War letters. I appreciate his guidance, which motivated me to complete *April's Revolution*.

A grateful thank you to all of my friends who reviewed sections of this manuscript: Kam Durham RN, Assistant Director of Nursing, Janet Eastman RN, MN, CRRN, NEA-BC, Dr. Peter Gutschenritter, Maranza Robinson BS, and Michael Shaffer, Assistant Director/ Lecturer at Kennesaw State University's Civil War Center.

A special thanks to Dr. Cedric Baker, Adjunct Clinical Assistant Professor of Pharmacy Practice at Mercer University for additional herbal research and medical utilization. His research greatly impacted the herbal study found within *April's Revolution*.

Saying thank you doesn't seem enough to Dr. Peter D'Onofrio, President of the Society of Civil War Surgeons. His countless hours examining drafts and providing Civil War medical data revealed his expertise and love for this subject.

Finally, my thanks and love to my husband (Dick Snoby) and our three children (Matthew, Andrew, and Bethany) who encouraged me throughout this three-year process. Dick was my biggest supporter both psychologically and financially. He never balked or gave me that "all knowing look" when I first told him I wanted to write a Civil War medical book. His faith in me never wavered.

DEDICATION

This book is dedicated to my ancestors: the Grahams, McKees, Iddings, Bennetts, Clarks, and Tobers. These patriotic men believed in our country and fought so that their children, grandchildren, and great grandchildren continue to live free.

PREFACE

I love history! I am enthralled with the people, places, and stories that are true and those that are legend. History excites my mind and demands for more details and experiences. I attribute my obsession of history first to my seventh grade teacher's Ancient World History class. There, I studied the Greeks, Egyptians, and Romans. She encouraged me to read Homer's *Iliad* and *Odyssey* and I was hooked!

My love-of-history frenzy really grew as my high school history teacher, Mr. Ellsworth Schwartz, introduced me to American history. As a class we made multiple field trips to French and Indian War battle sites where British General Braddock met his demise and George Washington surrendered Fort Necessity. Mr. Schwartz also diagrammed and explained battle strategies. These experiences fed my obsession.

When our family transferred from Pennsylvania to Georgia, I was exposed to living history re-enactments at the antebellum village of Roswell, Georgia. Love of history took a new turn and I began to give tours of Historic Roswell for the Roswell Historical Society and The Teaching Museum (North). Networking with Civil War re-enactors encouraged me to search archives and museums for information. Dispelling myths and exploring the truth drove me to begin a three-year quest resulting in *April's Revolution* (the title *April's Revolution* was chosen because the American Civil War had its birth and demise in that month).

I am not a college-educated historian. I am a registered nurse with a career in critical care, administration, research, program development, and evaluation. It is because of my medical background I am qualified to explore, question, and provide some insight into the medical practices and skills during America's history.

After achieving a master's degree in administration, organization, and operations research, I was honored with the first research award by Georgia Nurses Association as "Outstanding Nurse Researcher in Georgia." In *April's Revolution,* I applied those research skills by investigating the true medical care rendered during Colonial America, the American Revolution, Antebellum America, and the American Civil War. I found that care was based on race, economic status, and social status. Political philosophies, health care organizations, physician training, and medical/surgical treatments were examined by searching archived documents, personal letters, and secondary resources. Visiting museums, battlefields, cemeteries, and historical buildings added to my understanding, as did interviewing experts on various aspects of the Civil War. Each expert concentrated his expertise and interest within the Civil War, which added greatly to my knowledge and appreciation for their own love of history.

My research is comprised of primary resources existing within the National Archives, original soldier and surgeon diaries, medical collections, military writings, and old manuscripts dated from that era. Old city cemeteries, national cemeteries, and historical museum collections add surprising detail to augment the human suffering. Secondary sources of noted research professors specializing in African slave history and Internet sites with soldier's letters and information have added great substance to *April's Revolution.*

Several notable organizations provide rare information about the care of the sick and wounded soldiers. These organizations and their staff have been invaluable to my research: The National Civil War Medical Museum, Frederick, MD; National Museum of Health and Medicine, Silver Spring, MD; The Society of Civil War Surgeons, Reynoldsburg, Ohio; National Civil War Naval Museum, Port Columbus, GA; The Confederate Museum, Richmond, VA; Handley Regional Library's Stewart Bell Jr. Archive, Winchester, VA; Virginia Military Institute, Lexington, VA; Front Royal-Warren Rifles Confederate Museum, Front Royal, VA; Marietta Museum, Marietta, GA; Atlanta Historical Society, Atlanta, GA; and Georgia Historical Society, Savannah, GA.

Various drastic changes (revolutions) in American healthcare delivery happened during or soon after the war and continued into the 20th century. These advances are noted in *April's Revolution* within the nursing profession, research-based medical decisions, hospital and physician specialization, communication of information, organization by doctors, clinical usage of diagnostic equipment, approaches to disease management, and African slave healthcare. I am convinced that the war was the driving force that revolutionized American medicine in several ways and I hope you, the reader, will agree.

I have conveyed information that has long been forgotten but will prove of interest to living history re-enactors and Civil War enthusiasts. I am hoping that detail medical information will enrich their stories and demonstrations. Medical persons searching America's medical past will find new information to encourage their love of history.

INTRODUCTION

I always knew researching my family tree would be a long labor of love. I had no idea it would throw me into the American Civil War! It was only by accident I uncovered that five of my great-grandfathers fought for the Union. I knew that Patrick Graham of Johnstown, Pennsylvania, was my fourth great-grandfather from family documents and pictures. I researched Fold 3's database and found his service record as the captain of the 54th PA regiment who was killed at New Market Battle in 1864. This couldn't be true; I had a photograph of him as a much older man from the 1890's! After providing information to the National Archives, they corrected the error and presented me with his prisoner of war record after New Market. Enthralled and confused, my next step was going on multiple trips to Virginia's Shenandoah Valley and tracing Graham's journey.

New Market Battle is famous because of the role the Virginia Military Institute (VMI) cadets played in this Southern victory. Located within the Shenandoah Valley, I decided to explore the Virginia towns of Winchester, Front Royal, New Market, Lexington, Harrisonburg, and Staunton to find the truth about Graham. Gathering additional information from Richmond, the capital of the Confederacy, I was able to write about Graham's capture, medical care, and imprisonment. This information is found within his case study in *April's Revolution*.

I have thoroughly searched but have no claim on any family member fighting for the Confederacy. This is disappointing as one who has lived most of her life in the South. I have tried to be objective with my subject matter as one who was educated in the North and resides in the South. (I truly love Roswell and my Southern friends.)

April's Revolution begins with the state of health in early America. The white healthcare system emerges as early hospitals; theories of disease and treatments during the Revolutionary War era precede the care in antebellum America. The American Civil War demonstrates the growth of physician knowledge and beginning role of the professional nurse. I detail the care delivered to specific soldiers in a case study format and examine the common diseases, medical treatments, and trauma care experienced by the soldiers.

As I started researching materials for *April's Revolution*, I could not ignore the strong evidence that slave medical care was actually a different healthcare system than the one the white population experienced. It was important to understand and include this information in this manuscript. Several chapters detail the medical care provided as "Negro medicine" (a Southern specialty) given to the African slave of the South. Slaves were cared for in Southern slave infirmaries, medical school dispensaries, and plantation hospitals (sick houses). The slaves also had their own African folk doctors whose medical knowledge came from West Africa and/or the Caribbean. The individual slave performed self-care, which included herbal therapies adapted from American Natives or white doctors.

This new form of medical care not seen in the North arose only in the South. It was developed to support the Negro infirmaries and practiced by specialized Southern doctors, physician-partnerships, and Southern medical colleges. Some of the first experiments in America were performed on live slaves and forensic exploration on dead slaves in some of these medical school dispensaries. I believe that much of this information will prove surprising to the 21st century reader.

The care rendered to the white European race and the African slaves gave me insight into the 19th century political and social forces. These forces and previous methods of treatment impacted the Civil War's mortality and morbidity rates. What I learned encouraged me to develop a new approach to address the reasoning behind the medical methodologies and the role they played during the war. It is through a modern medical perspective that *April's Revolution* is different from other historical writings. This approach consists of modern scientific evidence, which disclaims or supports early medical premises concerning the racial intelligence, inferiority, and medical differences.

I used terminology in *April's Revolution* to describe the African slave, which was acceptable throughout the 18th and 19th centuries. The term "colored" was first used during the 14th Century for Sub-Saharan African ancestry peoples. The term has various meanings among many cultures. "Colored" first appeared in North America during the Colonial era. In 1863, the War Department established the Bureau of Colored Troops. "Negroe" was common in both the North and South during the 19th century. It wasn't until the 1910 U.S. Census that people of color were listed as Negroes, which continued until the 1960 Census. The term "black" was popular and continued until "African American" became widely used in the 1970's and "colored" was regarded as politically incorrect. For this paper, the term "colored" or "Negro" was incorporated as found among the researched historical documentation for accuracy. "African American" references 20th and 21st century people or medical care.

This manuscript describes the two healthcare systems in detail. However, *April's Revolution's* main goal is to reveal the many revolutionary changes and the beginning of America's modern healthcare system. (Part 9 details the major advancements or revolutions, which actually continued into the 20th century.) Many books and opinions were written declaring that horrific medical care existed during the Civil War. They told of uncaring and untrained doctors who were quacks doing amputations without anesthesia. It has only been within the last two decades that historians began to dispel these myths. *Aprils Revolution* is one document that supports the knowledge, concern, and skillful expertise of the Civil War doctor practicing under unimaginable conditions. They were doctors and nurses dedicated to providing the best care to soldiers.

PART 1

Health Problems in Early America

The early European settlers brought infections to the American continent. They feared the bubonic plaque and leprosy but these diseases remained in the old world. When the settlers arrived, there were few infectious diseases indigenous to America, thus they remained healthy for a time. The Native Americans were not so lucky. Many tribes were eliminated by smallpox, measles, and malaria, which arrived with the settlers. The European settlers had developed a partial immunity to these diseases but were disease carriers and that proved devastating to the susceptible natives.

Early colonial records record the settlers were poor and worked hard in this new land. Most 18th century families lived in self-contained rural units with minimal social interaction. Previously in the late 17th century, a law decreed towns with more than fifty families must educate the children. Public schools were established in one-room buildings throughout New England. This environment contributed to the spread of infectious diseases to the children, as did the ministers and doctors who brought organisms on their hands during visitations. (1) As little Johnny was sent off to school along with all of his friends, he returned home with scarlet fever or diphtheria infections to share with his family.

In New England, scarlet fever and diphtheria outbreaks occurred between 1735 and 1740 resulting in nearly half of the children dying. Women assumed the role of care giver/nurse to minister to families and neighbors. Various herbs and home remedies were utilized to provide cures, which sometimes did not work. Only religious nursing groups had specially prepared women with valid nursing skills and were sparsely located among certain urban areas.

Scarlet fever and diphtheria were not the only contagious diseases afflicting colonial populace. When the British left Boston in 1776 and traveled to the interior, an outbreak of smallpox went with the troops, proving that disease followed the military. During the Revolutionary War, General Washington ordered his soldiers at Valley Forge to be inoculated to protect against smallpox, which saved the Continental Army. Those soldiers were inoculated from scabs removed from infected smallpox victims. The infected debris was introduced into healthy soldiers by scratching the skin multiple times (enough to bleed), and applying part of the liquid scab into the wound. Most of the soldiers survived after a mild case of smallpox. Some inoculated soldiers perished after contracting the fatal form of the disease.

In the 18th century, quarantine of persons with infectious disease was the only alternative course of action. It was no surprise that quarantine laws developed beginning in 1755 for cities and ports. All doctors were required by 1796 to report any infectious diseases as they are today.

Imported contagious diseases such as yellow fever threatened seaports and spread to nearby towns. Isolation or quarantine of ships and sailors were early regulations to control disease. Inspectors detected obvious signs of contagious disease when the ships arrived in port. Even with these strict regulations, malaria and yellow fever became endemic along swampy river plains in the Southern colonies.

A new disease, cholera, entered the new United States in the 19th century and it soon reached epidemic status. Major cholera epidemics in 1832, 1849, and 1866 were seen among America's working class for many reasons. Prior to this, cholera was unknown in America, although it was prevalent in India. There was public outcry for the government to address cholera outbreaks, which led to the creation of local boards of health in the United States. (2) After the Civil War in 1866, New York City recognized that cholera outbreaks were preventable. Hence, it became accepted that health was the responsibility of the state government to enact legislation addressing health needs and rules. (3)

Disease and epidemics continued even with quarantine and state health rules. As populations migrated into the larger cities from rural areas, tuberculosis (consumption) became more common. There is much documentation that pulmonary tuberculosis remained the chief killer during the 18th and 19th century. Strangely, consumption was publicly viewed as a "romantic" affliction during the Victorian era.

PART 2

History of The American Hospital and The White Healthcare System

Wonderful little, when all is said.
Wonderful little our fathers knew.
Half their remedies cured you dead.
Most of their teaching was quite untrue.
Rudyard Kipling 1865-1936

CHAPTER 1

PUBLIC & PRIVATE HOSPITALS PRIOR TO 1800

Overview

The first hospitals appeared a century after the first English settlements developed. These hospitals were nothing like those we know today. General practice doctors had rare opportunities to specialize or develop surgical skills. Surgeries that were performed were always emergencies. The threat of infection was a constant. There was no way to deaden pain and control internal bleeding. As a result of these factors, there was no deep internal surgical manipulation within the chest and abdominal cavities.

The first American hospitals were built to contain the contagious diseases in early Colonial America. These "hospitals" were makeshift places located in New York, Philadelphia, Charleston, and Newport. Originally, there were two hospitals in the North: The New York Hospital and Philadelphia's Pennsylvania Hospital. The Pennsylvania Hospital was founded in 1751 due to the efforts of Benjamin Franklin and Dr. Thomas Bond. The Pennsylvania Hospital provided care similar to that of the New York Hospital.

> Not only did the hospital play a small role in the provision of medical care before the Civil War, it was in its internal structure a very different institution from that we know in the late twentieth century. The hospital was very much a mirror of the society that populated and supported it, a society rooted in deference and hierarchy, a society in which, traditional attitudes toward the responsibility of wealth were very much alive. Medical men needed and used the hospital; they could not control it. (1)

The New York Hospital was housed in 1771 at the almshouse, which provided care to the blind, insane, crippled, elderly, alcoholic, and those suffering from syphilis. Generally, those who went to the hospital had limited monies to pay for care or their families had abandoned them. The working class sought care only when they had extensive rheumatism, bronchitis, or pleurisy. Recovered patients played the role of nurses or attendants. Children were bedded throughout the New York City Hospital. Females and males were not separated from each other, nor were children from adults. (2) The American people did not consider hospitals as the primary source of care during the 1700s and early 1800s. The "respectable" people were treated in their homes when illness in the family occurred. The respectable woman would never be found in these facilities.

Continuous care facilities called almshouses were developed for the poor much later than the early hospitals. Their purpose was to provide medical care for the poor living in crowded cities. The first almshouse was built by William Penn to care for poor Quakers in 1713 Philadelphia. Urban workers who required more extensive care went to the almshouse, which had a medical staff. The indigent, insane, orphaned, and elderly were also housed in large city almshouses. The small cities had a local doctor who visited the chronically ill.

The mentally ill were sent to either the almshouse or prison. The first designated facility to care for the mentally ill was in 1772 at Williamsburg, Virginia, called the Eastern Lunatic Asylum. It did not admit incurable or contagious diseases. Not everyone found admittance. Potential patients had to be certified as morally worthy by the gentry's medical culture. Single pregnant women and those with any venereal disease were considered unworthy.

Both mental institutions and hospitals required permission for anyone desiring to be a patient. In the late 1700's, the Pennsylvania Hospital required a written document from a known respectable person stating the moral worth of the person seeking admittance. The medical staff consisted of elite doctors who answered to wealthy philanthropists who ran the facilities. These persons determined who was worthy to receive treatment. (3)

Philadelphia's Pennsylvania Hospital, pubic domain

The South had one hospital, Charity Hospital, located in New Orleans on Chartres and Bienville Streets in May 10, 1736. Originally it was named Hospital of Saint John and was the second oldest continuing public hospital in the United States. Charity Hospital relocated to Basin Street in front of St. Peter's Cemetery in 1743. After 1779's hurricane, the hospital was rebuilt in 1785 and called the San Carlos Hospital. It too suffered loss but this time the cause was fire.

By 1815, Charity Hospital was rebuilt on Canal Street in a swampy area. The hospital was in deplorable condition and patients suffered terribly. Steps were taken in 1829 to rebuild seeking income from the selling of slaves and hospital property. By 1832, a new building was created in time for the Sisters of Charity and Daughters of Charity to assume control of the hospital. Skilled nursing care finally arrived in New Orleans. (4) When hurricane Katrina struck in 2005, Charity Hospital closed. At this date, it is uncertain if it will be rebuilt or absorbed into a new university hospital project.

Specialized Care Hospitals

Colonial America organized temporary pest houses when smallpox epidemics occurred. These facilities continued throughout the Civil War era. During the 1700's, private inoculation hospitals were located outside of towns that provided smallpox inoculations.

There were many specialty hospitals opened during the 19th century. Religious groups, ethnic groups, masonic, and other benevolent societies created private philanthropic hospitals. Other specialized hospitals cared solely for a single disease, organ, or age group. These included tuberculosis sanitariums, eye disease infirmaries, deaf, blind and mute asylums, and insane asylums. America's first ophthalmic (eye), orthopedic (bone and joint), women (obstetric), and children's hospitals were founded in the 1850's for the urban poor.

As America became part of the Industrial Revolution, industrial hospitals developed as a direct consequence of economic growth. They provided care for workers where infirmaries and hospitals didn't exist. Some of these industries were Lowell Textile Corporation in 1839 and Central Pacific Railroad in 1869. Pennsylvania enacted legislation for local coal mining communities to aid particular industrial hospitals through subventions (grants from a government for financial aid to an educational institution).

Specialty hospitals flourished during the Civil War era. German and Jewish hospitals were built to care for immigrants who entered America in large numbers. Philadelphia founded a Jewish Hospital around 1864. The ethnic hospitals admitted chronic and elderly patients, which normally were excluded by other private hospitals. "Philadelphia's German Hospital founded in 1860-61 was sponsored by the German Society of Pennsylvania, J & P Baltz Brewing Co., Canstatter Volksfest-Verein, and the Cabinetmaker's Beneficial Society." (5)

Religious groups also established hospitals in America. Private hospitals regarded tuberculosis patients as difficult, unpleasant, and incurable. Cancer was seen as a disqualifier for admission and care.

Thus, religious institutions provided care for these individuals to comfort and alleviate suffering. Boston's Roman Catholic Carney Hospital reserved five floors for older patients who needed a home, who were not necessarily ill. New York's St. Luke's Hospital admitted chronic patients while "Episcopal laymen also saw to it that a Home for Incurables was established just outside the city." (6)

Prison Infirmaries

Both the English and the colonists housed the sick and injured with criminals in almshouses, mental asylums, and some local jails. Better times were ahead. The English Gordon riots of 1780 began in London as an anti-Catholic protest at the height of the Revolutionary War with America. European prison reforms arrived after the Revolutionary War and were adopted by the Americans. Some of these were separation of prisoners by sex, single cells, and separate infirmaries for criminal inmates.

> The Gordon riots resulted in the destruction of at least eight London prisons and houses of correction . . . further reforms came in 1784 with the passage of an act which required regular inspection of county gaols (jails), the segregation of prisoners by category, and the creation of separate infirmaries, chapels, and baths. Gaolers (jailers) were to be paid salaries and not live off the fees charged to prisoners, and liquor and gambling were prohibited. (7)

On April 5, 1790, the Pennsylvania legislature passed the law that established the legal foundation for America's first true prison system. This law provided guidelines for the Walnut Street Jail to confine the most hardened criminals. Its design became the model for all American prisons during the next thirty years. Meskell, who traces the rise of the penitentiary system in the United States from 1777 to 1877, mentions in the Standard Law Review that prison infirmaries exist but few details have been documented in other literature. (8)

Physicians visited the sick prisoners in jails and almshouses. Separate prison infirmaries didn't exist during these times. One of the widespread diseases of early colonial times was typhus, called hospital or jail fever. Dr. Benjamin Rush suspected lice carried typhus. Lice were found on blankets and clothing of persons who came to hospitals, prisons, and military camps. (9)

CHAPTER 2

MILITARY HOSPITALS

Army Convalescent Hospitals

When the Revolutionary War sailor became ill or wounded, he received care at a military or naval hospital. Once stabilized, these men filled the facilities to maximum capacity, preventing an open bed for the newly wounded or ill. An immediate place to recover from disease and injuries was needed throughout the colonies. The first convalescent hospitals in the United States were formed in September 1776 to serve the Continental Army and state militias. Connecticut was the first state to recognize the need to provide centers for recuperation of wounded soldiers. Small hospitals were set up with state funds in every town from "New Haven to King's Bridge New York." (10) Soldiers were sent to convalescent hospitals close to their own homes for further recovery. Once at home, the cost would not be on the Continental Army.

Military Hospitals

The first American military hospitals were established in public and private buildings for the acutely ill Continental military. Dr. L.G. Eichner in *The Military Practice of Medicine During the Revolutionary War* states that they were set up in barns, homes, huts, colleges, and churches. It was felt that the smaller the facility, the better. These facilities could not be called field hospitals but rather flying hospitals. The military, flying hospitals, functioned with a surgeon's table and emergency beds. This type of hospital was housed in tents or huts and located in protective sites with decreased exposure to invasive armies.

> They (flying hospitals) were located in relatively stable locations such as Providence and Newport, Rhode Island; Peekskill, Fishkill and Albany, New York; Hackensack, Fort Lee, Elizabeth, Amboy,

Brunswick and Trenton, New Jersey; Bethlehem, Bristol, Reading, Lancaster, Manheim, and Philadelphia, Pennsylvania; and Alexandria and Williamsburg, Virginia. (11)

While intentions were good, these hospitals provided a breeding ground for death and disease for the wounded, nurses, and doctors. The leading surgeon of the 1700's, Benjamin Rush, stated: "Hospitals are the sinks (latrines) of human life in the army. They robbed the states of more citizens than the sword."(12)

Confederate Surgeon General Samuel P. Moore later developed "Hospital Huts" during the Civil War. One wonders if this idea was forged from the flying hospital concept of the Revolutionary War fame. Eichner sees the hospital huts as precursors to the Korean War M.A.S.H. units.

Black Continental Soldier portrayed by John Elam, staff member, The Teaching Museum (North), Roswell, GA

Regimental hospitals were also developed, organized, and run by a regiment's doctors. Later, the regimental hospital existed in the early days of the Civil War and proved to be extremely inefficient and wasteful. They disappeared under Jonathan Letterman's plan.

Marine Hospitals

After the American Revolution, the new American government organized facilities to care for the ill and disabled seaman of the country. Previously, voluntary Marine associations in Boston and New York provided care for ill sailors.

Early Naval Legislation . . . the First American Navy

After the Revolutionary War, America was exposed to new conflicts occurring on the open seas. During 1785, Thomas Jefferson urged Americans that naval forces were required to protect passage in the Mediterranean from Algiers; but in August 1785, with no funds to support a Navy in the coffers, Congress had sold the last remaining ship in the Continental Navy.

Until 1797, the only armed maritime service was the Revenue Marine founded by Alexander Hamilton in 1790. Only when Algiers captured eleven more of our merchant ships in 1793, did Congress begin to take Jefferson's proposal seriously. France and Britain were also fighting a sea war at that time, which found our merchant ships harassed by both countries as well.

The Naval Act of 1794 was passed by the United States Congress on March 27, 1794 and established the first United States of America Naval force, which eventually became the United States Navy. With the adoption of this act, the construction of six frigates with an armed force began and the American Marines were born. (13)

America's second president, John Adams, signed into law the Act for the Relief of Sick and Disabled Seaman of 1798. This was done to ensure our national economic security and a strong national defense. The appropriated revenue was used to develop a national medical network to care for merchant mariners. This began the federal government's entrance into public medicine and disease prevention, which continues to this day. (14) This act caused rapid growth of the American Merchant Marine and expansion of our national commerce. The Federal government purchased Washington Point Hospital in Norfolk County from Virginia in 1801, to care for merchant seamen. After the American Civil War, this facility was no longer used as a hospital.

The Marine hospital system was felt throughout the country. "In busy ports, the government paid fees as necessary to individual doctors and boarding houses. In Massachusetts and Virginia, the federal government operated its own facilities; during the period between 1818 and 1860, the Marine hospitals served over 178,000 seaman." (15)

The Southern cities of Baltimore, Charleston, and the Northern city of Newport, Rhode Island, had early marine hospitals. In 1834, the City of Charleston operated a marine hospital at 20 Franklin Street. During the American Civil War, it treated Confederate wounded and seamen. During a Federal bombardment it became severely damaged; finally in 1933, the building was totally destroyed and never rebuilt.

Marine Hospital, Charleston, SC 1833,
courtesy of Library of Congress

Today's United States Merchant Marine is the fleet of the United States civilian-owned merchant vessels, which are operated by either the government or the private sector. It engages in commerce or transportation of services and goods in and out of our waters and is responsible for transporting cargo and passengers during peacetime. In time of war, it is an auxiliary to the Navy and can be called to deliver our troops and supplies for the military.

River Marine Hospitals

River city ports wanted their own marine hospitals. Natchez, Mississippi, petitioned Congress in 1802 for a marine hospital. The federal government agreed and created a marine hospital in New Orleans as well. Surprisingly, this occurred prior to the Louisiana Purchase. The government rented additional space from New Orleans' Charity Hospital. One year later, in 1803, the New Orleans Marine Hospital treated more than four hundred American sailors. (16)

Our country was expanding and river commerce became more important. In 1837, Congress authorized the building of the United States Marine Hospital in Louisville, Kentucky. Steamboats in 1840 dominated the river traffic fueling the country's industrial growth. Workmen from the Great Lakes, Ohio, and Mississippi River systems had injuries from engine or boiler explosions, collisions, wrecks, and freight handling. These boatmen were also exposed to environmental conditions leading to exposure to yellow fever, cholera, smallpox, or malaria. All mariners of every race received treatment, including free Blacks who worked as seamen. (17)

Custom officials examined sailors for eligibility to be treated at a mariner's hospital. The sailor must be a member of the Merchant Marine and currently paid hospital tax from his wages. Once qualified, the sailor made his way to the marine hospital. In some smaller ports, local residents housed the sick sailor and a local surgeon provided treatment. In 1884, the tax was eliminated but tonnage tax was created to maintain the Marine hospital system. From 1906 until 1981, Congress supported the marine hospitals with direct appropriations. The Marine hospital service became the Public Health Service in 1912 and changed to the Public Hospital Service Hospitals before closing in 1981. (18)

Naval Hospitals

Navy personnel received treatment at one of three naval hospitals operated by the United States Department of the Treasury. Congress specifically authorized these three hospitals located at Portsmouth, Virginia, the historic Boston district of Chelsea, and Washington City.

The cornerstone of the nation's oldest naval hospital was laid on April 2, 1827 in Portsmouth, Virginia, and began to treat patients in April 1830. Its first military casualties were from the Mexican American War. During the early days of the Civil War from 1861 to 1862, Portsmouth Naval Hospital came under the Confederacy's control. After the Battle Hampton Roads March 2, 1862, the hospital treated wounded and prisoners who survived the attack on the USS Congress and USS Cumberland by CSS Virginia. A national cemetery was located on the grounds with three hundred thirty-seven graves of those crew members. (19)

Portsmouth Naval Hospital

Chelsea Naval Hospital of Boston was commissioned and opened on January 7, 1836. The Chelsea Naval Hospital served naval personnel during the Civil War, Spanish-American War, World War I, and World War II. It originally had five historical buildings dating from 1836-1915 but more wings were added after the Civil War. The original naval hospital closed in 1974 and was converted into condominiums in 1980. (20)

The third hospital was the Old Naval Hospital on Pennsylvania Avenue in Washington D.C. When the Federal government moved to Washington City in 1800, the Navy Yard was providing medical services and supplies came from an apothecary shop located at the corner of 921 Pennsylvania Avenue and 9th street. The government built the Old Naval Hospital on this site. After being vacant for many years, The Friends of the Old Naval Hospital raised monies to restore the building to become a facility for education and community life on Capitol Hill.

**Present day photo of Old Naval courtesy of
Martha Boltz of the Washington Times**

On February 24, 1811, Congress passed an act to establish additional naval hospitals. The U.S. Secretary of the Interior temporarily leased wards during the Civil War at the Government Asylum for the Insane

(St. Elizabeth's). It wasn't until President Lincoln signed an act of Congress on March 14, 1864, one month prior to his assassination, to authorize the building of Washington's new naval hospital. The hospital opened in July 1866; the first patients were admitted on October 1, 1866 (one sailor and six marines). The first patient was a "colored ordinary seaman" wounded off the Texas coast. The first patient to die was a twenty-year old marine native of Germany with typhoid fever contracted on board a warship. In 1906, this new Washington Naval hospital moved to a new facility on Observatory Hill, 23rd Street and E Street, N.W. It became the Temporary Home for Veterans of All Wars in 1922.

PART 3

Medicine During the American Revolution

*These are the times that try men's souls: The summer
soldier and the sunshine patriot will, in this crisis,
shrink from the service of his country; but they that
stands it now, deserves the love and thanks of man and
woman. Tyranny, like hell, is not easily conquered;
yet we have this consolation with us, that the harder
the conflict, the more glorious the triumph. What we
obtain too cheap, we esteem too lightly . . . .*
Thomas Paine "Common Sense 1776

Recorded ancient history reveals that medicine had not changed
that drastically prior to the American Revolutionary days. Egyptian
medicine practices documented the first triage of care into three
categories: minor treatment, delayed treatment, intensive immediate
treatment. Drilling a hole into the skull was done to treat brain
injuries. A shunt (tube) was placed to drain air or excessive fluid
from the surrounding brain into the abdomen. Amputations were
performed for crushing injuries. These routinely occurred during
Egypt's pyramid building phase. Opium and beer were the anesthetics
used to decrease pain sensation in surgeries. As herbalists, Egyptians
had eight hundred and sixty prescriptions to use in their cures. Four
well-known medicines were aloe and turmeric for wound healing,
licorice to stop coughing, and frankincense to treat sore throat and
mouth ulcers. Dressings contained honey to fight against infection
and reduce swelling. American doctors used many of these treatments
during the 17th and 18th century.

Early American medicine reflected European science. A search for new drugs in America included those from the American Natives, resulting in scientific writings about the newly found flora and fauna. Herbal theories were tested and some discarded if they proved ineffective. African slave folk practitioners (doctors) brought many valuable plants and herbs from the Caribbean islands and West Africa. The main emphasis of medical disease theory and treatment remained based on those from Europe. (1)

CHAPTER 1
CAUSES OF DISEASE THEORIES

Body fluid balance theory was used in the European and colonial doctor practices; the Ancient Greeks developed this theory. They believed that keeping these "humors" balanced would result in good health. Balancing humors was done by removing the excessive body fluid through bleeding, purging, and sweating and with certain medications, specific foods, and rest.

As scientific theory grew, new theories concerning acidity, alkalinity, saltiness, tension and relaxation replaced the emphasis on humors. A noted physician of the mid 1700's discovered that muscle tissue contracted when enough stimulation was applied to that muscle's nerve supply. (Remember the frog experiment done in high school biology?) Based upon this finding, a new school of thought stated that nerve irritation could cause illness by altering the body's fluids. "Good health depended upon a proper balance of nerve stimulation to muscle and blood vessel response." (2)

These medical men believed there were many external stimuli that would excite the tissues to cause illness. Stimuli such as exposure to bad air, cold or heat, eating spoiled food, drinking contaminated water, and injuring the skin producing an open wound would result in sickness. Internal stimulation of muscles, nerves, and blood vessels would cause fevers, a fast pulse rate, and numerous body aches. The doctor diagnosed a state of excessive excitability when any of these stimuli became evident. (3)

By the time of the American Revolution, all illnesses were commonly thought to be caused by excessive nerve stimulation and cured with bleeding, surgery, a low diet, and whiskey or other spirits. The surgeon (doctor) would apply more stimulation by blistering the skin through "cupping" and the oral administration of purgatives, such as mercury and other caustic drugs as counter-irritant treatments.

Medical Treatments

The doctor's goal to remove excessive irritability relied upon bloodletting, blistering, rectal administration of medication (clysters), application of hot, wet substances (formentation), and use of various poultices (cataplasms). (4) Cataplasms, formentations, and clysters were simply different methods to administer the medications prescribed by the doctor. These all sound strange to us in the 21st century but every one of these practices was common. Most of the medicines used were to reduce fever, produce vomiting, relieve pain, and cause salivation, diarrhea, excessive sweating, and urination. The doctors were attacking the disease with everything they knew.

The 18th century doctor treated symptoms and not a specific disease, which included medications, that played a large role in his practice. The doctors erred in their use of medication by their selection of caustic substances and the amount and frequency of the medicinals administered. They thought if one dose caused improvement, more repeated and higher dosages of the medicine would cure disease. This was the beginning of heroic medicine, which resulted in a high death rate and horrible side effects for the patient.

Bloodletting was a simple method to remove excessive amounts of blood volume from the body. The doctor used a lancet or sharp knifepoint to cut through the skin into a large vein; today the procedure is known as venesection. This procedure was performed over and over within forty-eight hours until the desired results were achieved or the patient died from volume depletion and shock. Shock was not a rare occurrence.

Skin blisters were produced by the application of glass-like cups to the skin where an irritating substance had been placed. The skin under the cups would puff up with a blister filled with liquid and blood. These blisters were considered a counter-irritant to the disease excitability found elsewhere in the body.

When wounds occurred, 18th century doctors looked for pus as a stage in the healing process. Dr. Alfred Bollet's manuscript *Civil War*

Medicine Challenges and Triumphs, provides Civil War era information suggesting that there were two types of pus based on quality. Good quality localized pus was yellow, creamy and laudable caused by *staphylococcus* infections. The "malignant" pus was thinner with an offensive odor and caused by *streptococcal* infections.

Dr. Bollet's information is helpful to understand the thinking of the time, but today we know pus as a discharge found in infections and contains tissue debris, white blood cells and bacteria or other harmful organisms. Medical science examines and cultures the debris microscopically to determine the organism's sensitivity to antibiotic therapy. Culture and sensitivity of smear samples are routinely ordered; wound healing depends on an organism-free environment, no pus is a good thing.

Diet was an important part of all treatment plans. The much-used "low diet" consisted of a watery gruel of barley and a tea made from flax seed. Rum and whiskey were the "spirits" of choice given to stimulate the ill or invigorate the soldier after battle. Modern medicine knows that alcohol is a depressant and not a stimulant.

Theories of Healing

The Revolutionary War doctors believed that after a skin wound, a stage of inflammation set in on the third or fourth day. The signs of inflammation were pain, swelling, and heat. They thought that if the pain could be decreased then the bad inflammation could be prevented. Next, doctors used opium, purging, bloodletting, poultices, and warm baths to convert the pus or have the tissues absorb it. If this worked then the stage of digestion began when laudable pus was discovered in the wound. This "good sign" represented a form of excellent healing; an attitude which continued even to the early 1900's. During the digestive stage, injured tissues were sloughed off, leaving behind healthy tissue. (5) They were so wrong!

CHAPTER 2
SURGICAL TREATMENT OF WOUNDS

It was not unusual for a wound to be spouting blood from an artery. The doctors knew how to stop the bleeding with a needle and thread. If the artery was very deep and the doctor could not reach the bleeding vessel, he would use a compression bandage over the wound.

Burn wounds were common in the early days. Uniforms would catch fire and burns were treated with wine applications, which helped initially to prevent certain skin infections because of the alcohol content.

Many soldiers developed fractures from musket balls shattering bones with exit and entry wounds. Simple fractures were manually set and splinted with a pillow or plasterboard splints, and covered with leather sheeting. If the bone was sticking through the skin then there was no other recourse but amputation of arms and legs. This type of injury is called a compound fracture. Amputations were also done if certain conditions existed: if the patient was sent to an overcrowded hospital or if decay was already present. They knew and expected that the overcrowded hospital would likely cause widespread infections and patients would likely die from blood poisoning.

Head injuries were common in both the Revolutionary and Civil War. Skull fractures required trepanning (boring) into the skull bone to relieve blood or central nervous system fluid pressure, release of any pus found in the dura mater brain covering, or prevent a future hemorrhage into the brain. Twenty-first century medicine's burr holes are performed to release pressure and blood to prevent brain stem herniation and death of the patient. This procedure remains similar with more advanced high-speed drills under sterile operative conditions.

The doctor probed gunshot wounds with his finger and removed the musket ball with forceps, if it was within his reach. Next, he placed a lint dressing soaked in oil. A poultice of bread and raw milk was repeatedly applied to encourage healing. Keep in mind that milk was not pasteurized at this time and germs could easily invade the milk. Learning from the American Natives, the soldier's pain was treated with fever bark and opium in the form of laudanum. (6)

Chapter 3
Prevention of Disease

The major medical advance of the Revolutionary War era was personal hygiene and Continental Army camp sanitation. Dr. Benjamin Rush is credited with this achievement of encouraging personal hygiene and ordered the various camp sanitation methods. He temporarily acted as Washington's Surgeon General for the Middle Department in April 1777. During this time, he wrote a paper for the army officers on how to preserve the soldier's health. These recommendations included bathing two or three times per week and washing hands and face daily. Shaving daily and wearing hair short or plaited would help to prevent disease (lice infestation), besides looking neat and proper. Soldiers' shoes should be waterproofed with wax or they could use Indian moccasins, which were much warmer than leather shoes. (7)

Rush also recommended avoiding overcrowded living conditions; military hospitals were extremely congested with sick bodies. The recovering sick soldiers remained much too long in camp instead of being furloughed home. (8) As stated previously, this was the incentive to develop convalescent units close to the soldiers' own homes.

Recommendations for healthy camps were recorded by Dr. John Jones and included placing a tent on dry ground and avoid forest and marshes with damp air. Another recommendation was that straw bedding should be changed often and placed upon a waterproof cloth. Daily sunning of blankets was important. Jones also detailed ideal locations of soldiers' vaults (latrines) to prevent spread of the bloody flux (dysentery). (9)

The morbidity statistics for the troops was estimated to be eighteen percent during the entire war, with ninety percent of those becoming casualties. All soldiers feared typhus, typhoid fever, smallpox, and dysentery. The Southern soldiers were also exposed to malaria along with the diseases of the Northern soldiers. During and after the war, many soldiers returned home with their health permanently impaired due to chronic dysentery, rheumatic arthritis, tuberculosis, and heart disease problems.

Chapter 4
Revolutionary Military Hospital Overview

Early in the war, small houses became hospitals for the Continental Army's sick and injured. Soon, the numbers of soldiers were too numerous for these facilities. The medical consultants decided to turn to the British model of using larger buildings as military hospitals. One of the first was The Albany located in New York with forty wards. The Palace was the second one built at Williamsburg, Virginia. The towns of Peekskill and Fishkill in the Hudson River Highlands all had large hospitals.

By 1777, the Pennsylvania Hospital in Philadelphia expanded to include the almshouse to treat more soldiers. There were other large general hospitals in Bethlehem, Reading, Manheim, Lancaster, and Bristol, Pennsylvania that treated the military. New Jersey used hospitals in Hackensack, Fort Lee, Elizabeth, Amboy, Trenton, and Brunswick to aid the soldiers. Dr. Rush was not happy with the large hospitals' morbidity and mortality rates. He concluded that to be admitted to one of the army hospitals resulted in a twenty-five percent chance of death. (10) The doctors agreed that typhus could be due to the overcrowding in the hospital. The overcrowding was primarily because of the large number of convalescing soldiers. It was the military that requested each state develop small convalescent hospitals for troops returning home to recover. Those convalescing soldiers were instructed to return to duty once they were fit to fight again.

CHAPTER 5
CASE STUDIES

The following are two military/medical case studies about real-life revolutionary war patriots. One served with the 2nd Pennsylvania (PA) Regiment in New England and the other in the Southern colonies.

The 2nd PA Regiment was first established as a one-year enrollment on October 12, 1775 as the 1st PA Battalion under Col John Bull. The eight companies of the 1st PA Regiment participated in the unsuccessful attempt to capture Quebec in January 1776. The winter had taken its toll in sickness and exposure by March 30th, and the patriots abandoned the city to return to New York. Congress realized a larger national army was needed and increased enlistments to twelve months. This is when the 1st PA Battalion became the 2nd PA Regiment in 1776. (11)

Case Study of William L. Iddings

William L. Iddings was born in 1757 in Huntingdon County, Pennsylvania, and became a small time farmer in Chester County, PA. He enlisted on July 21, 1776 in Chester County as a private in the 2nd PA Regiment under Captain Thomas Miller and commanded by Col. John Bull.

After some training, the unit marched off to join other regiments on Long Island (NY). Here they fought the British at Flat Bush in Brooklyn from August 27-30, 1776. With the decisive British victory, Washington and the Continental Army retreated to Manhattan Island. Iddings was one of three thousand men under General Nathanael Green ordered to guard Washington's retreat at Fort Washington on upper Manhattan Island. British General Howe's forces planned to capture the fort, which was America's last stronghold on Manhattan. Washington issued an order for Greene to abandon the fort and remove the three thousand men across the Hudson River to New Jersey. Col. Robert Magaw, who was commanding the fort, refused to follow Green's order to abandon the fort to the British. He believed his men could successfully defend the fort from the invading enemy.

On November 16th, Howe attacked the fort on three sides. Surrounded by land and sea, the surrender of the fort became apparent, there was little Magaw could do. With Magaw's surrender, two thousand eight hundred and thirty-seven patriots became prisoners of war. After five months in the military, William L. Iddings was a twenty-year-old prisoner of the British. With this victory, the British continued to chase Washington's army across New Jersey into Pennsylvania. New York and eastern New Jersey were lost to the British.

Iddings contracted the bloody flux while on board one of the first British prisoner of war ships located in North River. (The North River is an alternate name for the southernmost portion of the Hudson River in the vicinity of New York City and northeastern New Jersey.) Iddings probably contracted the flux from the raw contaminated water drawn from the river and given to the prisoners to drink.

The British allowed prisoners to send and receive letters, buy or exchange for food, and possibly paroled. Private Iddings was one of those lucky few to be paroled on January 15, 1777. There is no record as to how this incident occurred, but probably due to excessive numbers of prisoners acquired from the ensuring battles with Washington's army, the British needed the room.

Without any money or supplies and in very poor health, Iddings was released to find his own way home to Chester, PA. Once home, the diarrhea and severe cramping were treated with opium, emetics induce to vomit, laxatives to create more diarrhea, and nourishing broths. After the emetics and laxatives had purged his system, and none were left to administer, Iddings had a better chance to survive with rest, nourishing food and a dry warm environment.

By May 1777, to fulfill his commitment, Iddings re-enlisted as a sergeant under Captain John Dougherty's Rangers, part of Col. Hunter's Invalid Corps. Their assignment was to defend the frontier of Northumberland, Northampton, Bedford, and Westmoreland Counties against the Indians who fought for the British. After several "brushes" with the Indians and nine months of service, Iddings was discharged in January 1778. He applied to Pennsylvania for a pension in 1833.

The earliest British ships were transformed into prisons. Previously, they were used to transport cattle and other supplies to support the British forces. They were decaying when the Patriot prisoners, from the battles at Brooklyn and Fort Washington, were confined in them. The ships included were the *Whitby, Good Hope, Scorpion, Prince of Wales, Falmouth, Hunter, Stromboli,* and *Jersey.* The *Scorpion, Strombolo,* and *Hunter* were designated as hospital ships. The floating prisons were originally intended to house captured seamen; some soldiers were sent to the ships when the land jails became overcrowded. The floating prisons in the Hudson did not require guards that land prisons called for; in fact, prisoners had no communication with the ship's crew. Americans also had prison ships in the Thames River at New London, Connecticut. British soldier POW's were also housed in copper mines near East Granby, Connecticut.

William L. Iddings survived two major battles, imprisonment, dysentery, enemy Indian attacks, and fourteen months of military service to marry and raise a family. (Iddings was my six times great-grandfather. He died in 1833 and lies buried in Butler County, PA.)

The British could have immediately executed the American prisoners of war. King George III had declared American forces to be traitors in 1775, and they would have been denied prisoner of war status. Fate stepped in, however, and early in the war Britain pursued a negotiated settlement with officials declining to hang the captured patriots. Hanging was the usual sentence for treason but the British did not want to insight public sympathy against the British who were stationed in America. The Continental Army captured British prisoners at the Battle of Saratoga and the British officials feared reprisals if captured American patriots were hung. This policy did not prevent the British from treating American prisoners more harshly than was standard for this time. The British neglected the prisoners who starved and slowly died of disease. Many POW's who did survive were permanently disabled from the lack of treatment for wounds and sickness.

Some historians report that there were ten thousand American POW's: four thousand from battles around New York, five thousand from battles in the South, and one thousand from naval combat. New York City was one of several sites where American prisoners were held. Charleston's sugar cane houses were also used by the British as POW prisons. The Continental Army was permitted to supply the prisoners. This was not often done since even the army was experiencing shortages of food to feed the fighting soldiers.

Once the prisoner population became unmanageable, the British used obsolete, captured, or damaged ships as prisons. More Americans died of neglect than were killed in battle. There were sixteen hulks that served as prison ships off the Brooklyn coast and they remained throughout the war. Some of the POW bodies were tossed overboard and others buried in shallow graves along the coastline. Over the years, many of those remains were washed up and recovered by residents. These remains were interred in the Prison Ship Martyrs' Monument at Fort Greene Park, part of the Long Island battlefield. (12,13,14)

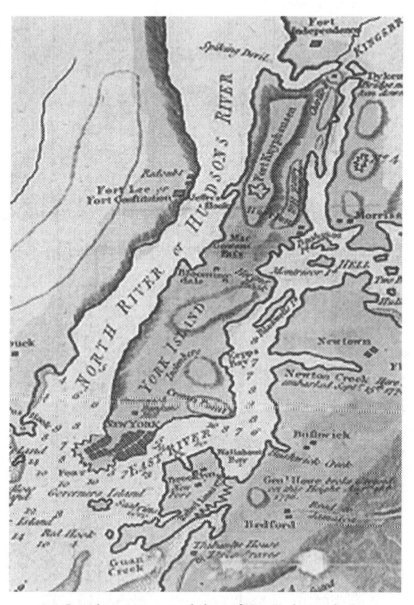

1781 British map & nautical chart of New York & its harbor,
courtesy Norman B. Levinson Map Ctr., Boston Public Library

Case Study of John Whelchel

John Whelchel was born on October 11, 1756 in Albemarle County, Virginia. He enlisted at the age of twenty-one under Captain James Steen and Col. John Thomas on May 25, 1777, while residing in South Carolina. He fought in the Southern colonies at the battles of Kings Mountain, Blackstock's Plantation, Rocky Mount, and Fishing Creek. Whelchel received a saber wound resulting in four cuts on the head, a depressed skull fracture, and three or four stab wounds of the body at the Battle of Cowpens.

Family stories related how Whelchel's three brothers, comrades in arms at Cowpens, found John on the battlefield. Their father, Dr. Francis Whelchel Sr., treated young Whelchel's injuries by making a silver plate for the soldier's fractured skull out of melted silver coins. The silver plate was placed over the exposed brain tissue, saving John's life. After recovering from his wounds and surgery, he joined Capt. Robert Montgomery and Col. Brandon in the battle at Eutaw Springs. After the war, John resided in Hall and Gilmer Counties, Georgia, and received a pension in September 1832. (15)

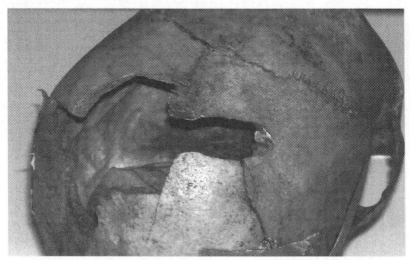

Depressed skull fracture struck by an object, author's picture

After the Battle of Monmouth in New Jersey on June 28, 1778, the war front shifted to the South. The Southern Tories were very strong in the South and the British held the Georgia and South Carolina coastal areas. On January 17,1781, General Daniel Morgan's Americans performed an amazing victory over Tarleton's British legion at Cowpens, South Carolina. The battle lasted only one hour resulting in one hundred and ten British killed, two hundred wounded, and five hundred taken as prisoners. Three hundred of the British were able to escape. The patriots lost with twelve men killed and sixty wounded. Cowpens was the beginning of a long list of British disasters that year. British victories were costly at Guildford Court House and Eutaw Springs with one thousand British soldiers killed or wounded. Cornwallis, a British commander in the South, decided to focus on Virginia and marched off to Yorktown. The rest is history.

PART 4

Antebellum Medicine (1800-1860)

*A pioneer is generally a man who has outlived his
credit or fortune in the cultivated parts.*
Dr. Benjamin Rush, 1787

Dr. William Buchan was born in 1729 in Southern Scotland. In 1790, he presented a thesis to British doctors on preventing and curing diseases using strict regimens and medications. His main points summarized how European and American medicine viewed disease on the eve of the 19th century.

> Unwholesome air is a very common cause of disease . . . Air may become noxious in many ways. Whatever greatly alters its degree of heat, cold, moisture renders it unwholesome. (1)

The impact of his theory called for free air circulation in houses, churches, infirmaries, city streets, and bedchambers. He even criticized the burial of bodies within churches, churchyards, and nearness to cities. He was convinced the rotting of the bodies contaminates the air:

> Certain it is, that thousands of putrid carcasses, so near the surface of the earth, in a place where the air is confined, cannot fail to taint it and that such air, when breathed into the lungs, must occasion disease. (2)

Buchan strongly stated that infection doesn't always die when the patient dies. Everything the patient touched was contagious such as clothes, blankets, and body fluids. Therefore, the dead should be buried quickly and far from the populace. Infected persons should be kept a long distance from the healthy as a means of preventing infection or defilement.

Buchan praised the use of ventilators to expel foul air as the "most useful of all our modern medical improvements." (3) He also strongly supported cleanliness with ventilated air to preserve the health of mankind. Ventilators were special openings on roofs to allow bad air out and good air into the building. Windows and doors were also considered good ventilators.

He suggested that the spread of infectious diseases would be dramatically reduced if there were proper nurses to care for the sick. Caregivers should:

> Stuff their noses with tobacco or some other strong smelling herb, as rue, tansy or the like. They ought likewise to keep the patient very clean, to sprinkle the room where he lies with vinegar, or other strong acids, frequently to admit a stream of fresh air into it, and to avoid the smell of his (the patient) breath as much as they can. (4)

Dr. Buchan's treatise has some common sense elements including frequent hand and face washing, wearing clean clothing, exercising, and eating nutritious foods. It is true that certain infections are spread in the air while others are carried on clothing, food, and other items. Not all organisms are transmitted through these vehicles but 18th and 19th century medicine stressed that "bad miasma" was the sole entity behind infections transmission.

The fear of bad miasma continued to reign through most of the 19th century until Lister's germ theory became accepted. Florence Nightingale was the most outspoken crusader supporting the bad air theory and need for cleanliness in hospitals, camps, food, water, and personal hygiene of soldiers. Her skill as a statistician gave quantifiable evidence that supported her theories and methods used during the Crimean War, which saved many lives. Perhaps she was influenced by Dr. Buchan's treatise.

Medical men were very committed to care for the American soldier during the Revolutionary War. By the war's conclusion, they were optimistic about the country's future, especially what they had learned about military medicine. The country was now freed from the old European medical systems that were not helpful in treating America's diseases. The 19th century ushered in the Victorian Age along with an unrealistic romantic approach where phrenology became vogue. It appeared as one of many pseudo-scientific doctrines held in this age.

> All problems could be solved by some adventurous, new solution which promised the millennium . . . health, inevitably was central to some of these programs . . . after being rejected in scientific circles in 1780's, it continued to attract popular attention during the next century and apparently played a part later in the origins of Christian Science. (5)

The 1800-1840's were known as the "Paris School" medicine era where empirical philosophy, physical sciences, and surgical structures became popular. Systematic medical research, which correlated clinical and pathological findings, found its way from Europe to America. American doctors, from large city hospitals, were strongly influenced by the British and French ideas. Many American student doctors extended their knowledge by attending graduate medical studies in Paris or London. Almost seven hundred Americans studied medicine in Paris with ten percent returning to teach in American medical schools. (6)

The introduction of additional clinical observation tools of the pulse watch, clinical thermometer, stethoscope, and microscope were found throughout urban America. Doctors began to examine patients with these tools. Facts supporting diagnosis and treatments were being required rather than trial and error observations and treatments as in the past.

Physiology of nerves and anatomical function were taught using systematic animal experiments. Medical students began to observe autopsies on human bodies. Physician surgical expertise and intervention grew more popular with the focus on pathologic anatomy. With the discovery of sulphuric ether in 1842 by Dr. Crawford Williamson Long of Franklin, Georgia, surgical intervention enabled doctors to perform more technical and major (deep tissue) operations. (7) Dr. Morton of Massachusetts experimented with chloric ether and published in the "Boston Medical and Surgical Journal of Nov. 18, 1846." (8) The controversy over who really was the "Father of Anesthesia" began and continues to this day.

Mental health was addressed through more humane and psychological approaches as the majority of states subsidized insane asylums. Electric shock therapy (EST) would clinically appear as a new medical treatment in the 1860s. During the 21st century, EST has again become a recognizable therapy, especially for depression.

The prescribing of medicines and herbs by the trial and error method became obsolete. Doctors used caustic drugs that included arsenic, mercury, and chlorine to rid the body of bad "humors." The puke and purge practices could easily result in severe levels of dehydration, electrolyte imbalance, and even death. The most noted drugs used for this practice was Calomel, a mercury compound and tartar or ipecac. Other forms of purging utilized laxatives containing arsenic. While arsenic caused expected vomiting and diarrhea, it's other adverse conditions such as heart disease, neurological dysfunction, gangrene of the mouth and face, and even cancer were possible.

Doctors knew that opium and morphine were addictive producing a tolerance to certain drugs with chronic usage. Addictive drugs were freely given without understanding the ultimate consequences and sequel. Morphine injections using hypodermic needles and widespread adoption of quinine to control malarial fevers were two of many new pharmaceutical advances. Both white people and slaves were given the same drugs and treatments by white doctors, plantation masters and mistresses, and overseers. They studied dosages and regulated drugs according to age, weight, sex, and race of the patient. (9) As the 1850s approached, heroic therapy was the "gold standard for medical treatment" and bloodletting and cupping were slowly being abandoned. Bleeding promoted a release of blood, which could result in a dangerously low level of blood volume and death. A consequence of long-term cupping was the breakdown of the body's first line of defense the skin. Once open sores developed, infection was very likely to occur, this depended on the patient's resistance. Antibiotics were not yet discovered and few antiseptic solutions were used to effectively treat severely infected wounds caused by the cupping.

By the mid-1850s, doctors performed smallpox vaccinations, superficial operations, and set fractured bones. They performed some difficult child birthing procedures, although midwives were always sought first during labor and delivery.

Every American doctor was a combination physician, surgeon, and apothecary in the 1700s. As medical specialties developed, American medical colleges changed their methods and produce doctors who wanted graduate training as specialists in surgery or ophthalmology. These men and a few women struggled for professional identity through professional medical organizations and publications. (10)

PART 5

The African Slave Healthcare System

*No man can put a chain about the ankle of
his fellow man without at last finding the
other end fastened about his own neck.*
Frederick Douglass

Chapter 1
The Middle Passage

The height of the Atlantic slave trade occurred between 1700 and 1800. This was when the majority of captives were brought from the shores of Africa to the new world. There were at least fourteen colonial slave ports that sent and received ships to bring the African slaves to America; the majority was from the Northern colonies.

Over the almost four hundred years of the slave trade from the late 15th to the late 19th century, 12.4 million souls were loaded onto slave ships and carried through the Middle Passage across the Atlantic to hundreds of delivery points which stretched over thousands of miles. (1)

The crossing was fraught with incredible danger for both the crew and the captured cargo, the Africans. Not only were these people torn from their homes but their heritage, customs, traditions, way of thinking, and behaviors were in danger of annihilation. Their immediate need was survival from the exposure to the harsh elements found at sea, disease, infections, and dehydration. These would be the first battles fought on board ship.

The African's existence depended on medical care from a European or American ship doctor, but there were few ship doctors in the early 18th century. Ship captains used a recipe book for medicines to treat any problem, if he could recognize the symptoms. Later, ship doctors accompanied most voyages. Yet, many Africans did not survive the voyage, death came from measles, smallpox, tuberculosis, or influenza. The Africans had little or no immunity to these European diseases. The greatest killer during the Middle Passage was bacterial or amebic dysentery, which was called the bloody flux. (2, 3) Medical men lacked the skill and equipment to recognize what caused the disease, the prevention of disease, or the correct treatment. Only symptoms were recognized and treatments were a result of trial and error.

Slave ships arriving with crew or passengers having symptoms of smallpox were quarantined on board up to four months. Quarantine proved very costly to the slave merchants. These men tried to prevent outbreaks by inoculating slaves with smallpox vaccines in Africa before sailing to America. Yet, after arrival, many of the enslaved Africans continued to die from something else. Africans died as a result of severe diet changes, hard labor, differences in climates, and exposure to an environment conducive to infectious diseases.

Northern and Southern slave merchants and owners adapted a process called "seasoning" to decrease the large number of slaves from dying. Seasoning was first introduced during the colonial era when the new immigrants arriving in America became ill and died at alarming rates. Proper seasoning would take about three years to complete. This process consisted of gradually introducing American foods into the slave's diet, providing warm clothing and blankets in winter months. They also decreased the slave's number of work hours per day from the regular fourteen to ten or twelve hours. They also provided less stressful tasks until the slave became fully acclimated.

It was important to season the slave; it was estimated that fifty percent or more perished before three years after capture. (4) The seasoning would start over again when slaves were sold and transported farther inland from the coastal plantations to more temperate climates.

Sickness and injuries were bound to occur among the millions of enslaved Africans, resulting in a need for more, as well as better, medical care throughout the South. The African slave residing in the South received medical care through four entities: slave infirmaries owned by doctors, medical school dispensaries, plantation sick houses, and municipal commercial hospitals. They comprised the second healthcare system in America.

Chapter 2

Doctoring the African Slave

Southern doctors were trained in various modes of learning such as apprenticeships, homeopathy, Thompsonian, and allopathy to name a few. Most wealthy Southern sons desiring to become doctors attended Northern college medical schools or traveled to European medical centers of knowledge located in Paris or London. That was about to change in the first half of the nineteenth century. In order to grow the reputation of the Southern physician and medical schools, sound clinical practice and a reputable college medical education were the keys to accomplish this goal. The desire to be recognized among their medical peers here and abroad partnered with the need for slave medical care resulted in the private slave infirmary.

One can see the early beginnings of the African slave's healthcare system taking shape first on the Southern plantations. Most large Southern plantations had some form of medical facility to maintain the health of their slaves. Some of the more famous plantation slave hospitals were located at Melrose Plantation in Natchitoches Parish, Louisiana; Retreat Plantation on St. Simons Island, Georgia; Poplar Hill Plantation Clinton, Maryland; and Somerset Place Plantation Creswell, North Carolina. Many smaller plantation owners chose to treat their slaves and care for them in the slaves' quarters. The owners used Southern doctors who had knowledge of a new type of medical care called Negro medicine.

With the adoption of the slave infirmary as a business enterprise, another faction of the slave healthcare system evolved. Private infirmary staff cared for slaves in Southern urban centers in the 1800s; these facilities were owned and operated by doctors and Southern medical schools. They grew rapidly and by the 1840s were found in South Carolina, Georgia, Mississippi, Alabama, Tennessee, Virginia, and Louisiana.

Melrose Plantation Negro Hospital, Louisiana.
Author-purchased photograph

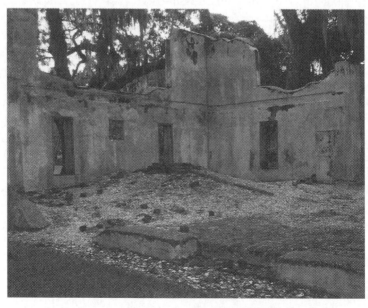

Retreat Plantation Slave Hospital, St.
Simons Island, author's photo.

In the beginning, the slave infirmaries were built as quarantine stations or pest houses. That changed when the importation of slaves ended in 1807. The value and demand for more slaves increased within America with the invention of the cotton gin, as did the demand for the slave infirmary to treat and season slaves for the owners and slave merchants. (5) The value of slave infirmaries in towns along railroads, river ways, and in land routes grew to answer the demand for preventative slave medical care. The infirmaries continued to provide for seasoning of those slaves who were sent from the coast to the interior.

The most famous land route was the Natchez Trace, a historical path about four hundred and forty miles between Natchez, Mississippi, and Nashville, Tennessee. It linked the Cumberland, Tennessee, and the Mississippi Rivers. Later, Thomas Jefferson decreed that the country needed a postal road between Daniel Boone's Wilderness Road and the Natchez Trace. Once constructed, this new route allowed slaves to be transported from Baltimore and Alexandria, through (West) Virginia along with slaves from Richmond, and travel on to Nashville, Memphis, Natchez, and New Orleans.

**Natchez Trace at Belle Meade Plantation
Nashville, TN, author's photo**

Dr. Kenny documents that a slave infirmary existed on the Natchez Trace known as Henderson and Nash Negro Infirmary of Kosciusko, Mississippi (Hometown of Oprah Winfrey of TV fame). The sick or injured slave traveling to Natchez or New Orleans received emergent but rudimentary medical care there. Many slaves would have perished along the long journey without this type of medical intervention, and the slave merchant/speculator would have lost his investment. Slave owners were very willing to pay for medical assistance to assure his slave merchandise was in a healthy state.

A remote slave infirmary was located on the South Carolina railroad between Charleston and Augusta known as the Blackville Infirmary for Negroes. Dr. W.W. Smith treated chronically ill slaves from surrounding plantations and performed any emergency surgical procedures that the slaves required. Since Blackville's infirmary was conveniently located on a main transportation line, it provided medicines and simple surgeries on the transported slaves. This service ensured the slaves would arrive healthy at the two main Southern auction sites of Augusta, Georgia, and Charleston, South Carolina.

The majority of doctor owners of the slave infirmaries were men of renowned medical reputation. The majority of these men believed in the institution of slavery and its value to the South during the antebellum era. This aspect of the slave healthcare system provided good medical care for this time in history; it was not medicine as we know it today. To many of the doctors, their goal was to earn a living, but there were a few who wanted to advance the Southern medical profession's reputation and research knowledge.

The infirmaries were mostly staffed by one doctor and at least one nurse who dispensed medicines to the slaves. The staff developed individualized medical plans of care and performed surgical procedures as needed. They supplied appropriate measures to safeguard slaves from running away. One fee per week included the medicines, food, and lodging for the slave. The doctor performed surgical procedures on slaves that were approved by the slave owner. The slave was not required to give his consent. If the slave recovered from the surgery, the doctor's reputation then spread and his wealth increased. If the slave died, the autopsy would add to the doctor's knowledge base and the medical community, once the case was published in a professional medical journal. If the slave died, the owner was not required to pay for the procedure or the slave's burial. How comforting this was for the slave's family!

The medicines and treatments given at the infirmaries (bloodletting, puking, and purging) were the same that whites endured. Later, certain doctors began to specialize in Negro medicine. These doctors believed that, medically, the African could not tolerate the result of zealous decrease of blood volume and dehydration. The volume depletion resulted from the bloodletting, vomiting, and extensive diarrhea inflicted by the caustic drugs. Not everyone adopted this medical approach to ban these procedures given to the slave, but they certainly adopted the implications that supported slavery. Those assumptions were proved to be true with time.

Negro medicine's foundation was based on the theory that there were further physiological differences between whites and African slaves. Many of these doctors manipulated their medical findings to support slavery and the attitude that the African race was inferior. They claimed Africans could better endure heat and had thicker skin than whites. These findings supported that Africans were ideal for fieldwork in the hot climates of the South. It was apparent that Africans had odd-shaped heads and must therefore be intellectually inferior. They were lazy and unable to provide food and shelter for their own survival, if left on their own.

Other medical specializations were slowly becoming a reality. Doctors who wanted advanced European training returned home with new skills and ideas. One such entrepreneur was Dr. Francis Peyre Porcher of South Carolina. After graduating from the Medical College of the State of South Carolina, he furthered his education in Europe with a specialty in ophthalmology. In 1850, Dr. Porcher opened an ophthalmic Negro infirmary in Charleston, South Carolina.

Dr. Porcher, courtesy of National Library of Medicine

In 1852, Porcher opened the Charleston Preparatory Medical School of the Medical College and lectured on *materia medica* and therapeutics. *Materia medica* is a Latin term for the body of knowledge about therapeutic properties of botany and pharmacology.

By 1855, he and Dr. Julian Chisholm opened another Negro infirmary in Charleston. During the Civil War, Confederate Surgeon General Moore assigned Porcher to investigate various alternative plants grown in the South. Moore was hoping to augment the Confederacy's depleting supply of medicines, since the Union blockade prevented drugs from entering the South. There were a limited number of drug-producing laboratories in the South that could not meet the increasing demand. Porcher wrote *Resources of the Southern Fields and Forests, Medical Economical, and Agricultural Botany of the Southern States*, but it proved a little late to help the Confederacy. (6)

Dr. Chisholm, courtesy National Library of Medicine

Dr. Julian Chisholm, born in Charleston, SC, graduated from the Medical College of the State of South Carolina, and spent two years studying eye surgery in Parisian hospitals. He then traveled to Milan, Italy, to observe the surgical treatment of wounded soldiers at Magenta and Solferino during the Austrian and Italian war. The knowledge Chisholm gained from his European experience would serve him well in the coming American Civil War. Most Civil War enthusiasts recognize his name as author of the *Manual of Military Surgery*. This manuscript contained written surgical guidelines for the Confederate doctors who had little or no military surgical experience. (7)

In Augusta, Georgia, doctors from the Georgia Medical College opened two slave infirmaries. As faculty members, the motivation to own these infirmaries was more academic than to supplement their salaries; one of the infirmaries was located on Jackson Street.

The Campbell brothers, Drs. Henry F. and Robert, built the Jackson Street Hospital and Surgical Infirmary for Negroes in 1854. Its mission was to care for slave and free colored with long-term medical needs from the surrounding plantations and towns. The hospital was a three-story building located on Jackson (Eighth) and Fenwick Streets in Augusta, Georgia, with sixty to seventy beds.

> With use of ropes and pulleys, patients could be transported to upper-floor rooms from the operating room. Rooms were equipped with gaslights, fireplaces, and hot and cold water. (8)

The hospital was regarded as an extremely modern and forward-thinking center. It is rare to find an actual picture of a slave infirmary; the following picture of Jackson Street Hospital is one thought to be the ideal modern facility. The hospital was extremely important to Augusta prior to and during the war. (Today, housing units occupy the hospital site that once had served the slave population.) Augusta was a booming industrial site on the Augusta canal and Savannah River. It received cotton field barges for market from South Carolina and Georgia and was the primary producer of powder and ammunitions for the Confederacy.

JACKSON STREET HOSPITAL,

AND

SURGICAL INFIRMARY,

FOR NEGROES,

AUGUSTA, GEORGIA.

**Dr. Paul Eve courtesy of Historical Collections
& Archives, Robert B. Greenblatt, MD Library,
GA Health Sciences University**

Dr. Paul F. Eve, another infirmary owner, received his degree from the University of Pennsylvania and then studied in Europe. He opened his Negro surgical infirmary near the Medical College of Georgia in Augusta. The infirmary was part private hospital and part teaching facility. Eve served the college as dean for eight years and editor of the *Southern Medical and Surgical Journal* for five years. He was considered a respected member of the medical profession. (9)

Old Medical College of GA. Courtesy of Historical Collections & Archives, Robert B. Greenblatt, MD Library, GA Health Sciences University

New Orleans was the Southern center for growth of slave infirmaries. Louisiana and Mississippi plantations provided many ill or injured slaves who required medical care in New Orleans. The seaport brought hundreds of ill slaves to the infirmary doors as well. The slave population suffered from cholera, smallpox, and yellow fever in greater numbers than the whites. They also experienced a harsh climate under dangerous working conditions on the sugar cane plantations. Some of the infirmaries did not have proper separate wards for infectious cases so they refused to care for them. Subsequently, the contagious slaves were sent to Charity Hospital for treatment and quarantine.

CHAPTER 3
COMMERCIAL SLAVE HOSPITALS

One more segment of the slave healthcare system developed hospitals operating as commercial businesses. They were larger than infirmaries and offered more services to its clientele. New Orleans hosted the most number of commercial slave hospitals in the South. By 1810, New Orleans was the fifth largest American city. A young Jewish man, Judah Touro, made a fortune based on the shipping business here. With his fortune, he decided to establish a clinic and infirmary to serve the unfortunates of New Orleans and the mariners who entered the port. The Touro Infirmary/Hospital was located in the center of the city's shipping activities near the steamboat landings in the twenty-four bed Paulding mansion. The first house surgeon and administrator was Dr. Joseph Bensadon, a Jewish Doctor born in New York who graduated from Charleston University. (10)

Slave admissions were the mainstay of the Touro infirmary from 1855-60. Dr. Bensadon also provided warranties or certificates of "soundness" so that the traders could sell their slaves. It was well known that many New Orleans slave traders regularly sold unhealthy slaves to planters. The Louisiana legislators created redhibition laws to counter the many complaints of the planters. The redhibition laws permitted the buyer to return a slave (the product) if the slave proved unhealthy before one year after purchase. These laws enabled Dr. Bensadon to subsidize his income with his medical testimony of "slave soundness" for insurance companies.

Touro Infirmary was in the perfect location to receive the slaves brought ashore at the waterfront wharf. The slaves needed to be "seasoned" and treated prior to sale at the auction block. Slaves were shipped chained together in tight quarters, and arrived in poor physical condition. They had contracted fevers and become exhausted and dehydrated from the long voyage along America's coastline. Most of the slaves were treated and revitalized at Touro Infirmary or at Hotel Dieu, opened by the Sisters of Charity. (11)

Charity was the oldest hospital in the South but was never considered a hospital that treated African slaves. It served mainly the white and poor; however, slaves were only admitted if they had contagious diseases and were placed in quarantine. The hospital did offer medical students an ample number of bodies (poor whites and slaves) each day for dissection purposes. (12)

Chapter 4
Medical Schools' Dispensaries

The dispensary was an invention of the British as a freestanding alternative to a hospital, where the poor could receive medical care. It resembled today's ambulatory outpatient surgical center. By the 1800's, the dispensary was a facility where advanced clinical medicine was taught to doctors who wanted to gain additional experience, similar to modern day residency programs. (13)

Medical school dispensaries proved to be the academic and research components of the slave's healthcare system. The Negro dispensary treated both slave and freed blacks of urban areas.

As a patient at the dispensary, if the slave expired, the body had further use in education and research for the staff. The slave's family was not required to give consent for the post-mortem care or disposal. Archaeological excavations confirmed that extensive practice of using slave bodies for anatomic research and dissection existed at the medical schools. (14)

Negro dispensaries were located at the Medical College of Georgia in Augusta, the Medical College of South Carolina, Charleston; the Medical College of the State of South Carolina, Charleston; and the Richmond's College Infirmary of Hampden-Sydney Medical Department (later Medical College of Virginia). They became the foundation of Negro medicine. (15) The dispensaries were a valuable component of the African slave's healthcare system. Negro medicine used trial and error philosophies to determine which treatment methods would work best on slaves. Only a few doctors claimed specialization in this field prior to the Civil War. Negro medicine philosophies continued to grow through reconstruction and beyond. These slave infirmaries closed due to the war. It took many years to prove or disprove these theories, and racial prejudice accompanied some of the treatment approaches.

Validation of certain aspects of Negro medicine occurred through legitimate research methods of the 1950s and 1960s. They revealed why the West Africans were immune to a deadly type of malaria and why many children of African descent didn't survive their teenage years.

The doctors, educated in Southern medical schools, wanted to elevate the Southern medical profession's reputation. They knew that extensive clinical training using diagnostic tools on the living and dissecting cadavers became a priority to achieve this goal. (16) The study of human anatomy was surfacing in early 19th century America. The best method to learn anatomy was to examine the internal organs through manual exploration of dead bodies, and then relate findings to clinical practice. Most early Americans were horror stricken about the post-mortem cutting of a loved one's body. Therefore, a shortage existed to study the anatomy of cadavers throughout the South.

To solve the shortage problem, both medical students and doctors acquired cadavers through grave robbing of criminals, poor whites, slaves, and free colored. The medical students became known as "Resurrectionists" or "grave rats". The Scottish were the first to fear grave robbers and that fear migrated to the people of the new world. Families placed iron bar fencing to guard graves, in order to keep the body snatcher from performing their livelihood. (17) The very old cemeteries still remaining show the iron workings around family plots.

> *"The Body snatchers! They have come*
> *And made a snatch at me;*
> *It's very hard them kind of men*
> *Won't let a body be!*
> *Don't go to weep upon my grave*
> *And think that there I be;*
> *They haven't left an atom there*
> *Of my anatomy"* by Dr. James Craik, physician to
> George Washington (18)

One of the most famous body snatchings was done in full daylight at Harpers Ferry. Some of Winchester Medical School Academy's students were at the arrest of John Brown's terrorists in 1859. They found a dead man stretched out on the bank of the Shenandoah River at Harpers Ferry. After placing their lucky discovery in a box, it was shipped to the academy. Upon opening the box in Winchester, papers revealed the body was one of John Brown's sons, as the story was told. Nonetheless, the body was used for dissection and teaching purposes for several years. When the war came to Winchester, Union General Nathaniel Banks occupied the town in the spring of 1862. Banks heard rumors about the body of the Brown boy and he sent soldiers to the academy. The Union soldiers discovered the labeled skeletal remains in the academy basement. General Banks sent the body to the North for proper burial and ordered the academy building to be burned. (19)

State legislations forbid the practice of body snatching so a lawful procurement method was required to obtain cadavers for educational purposes. Conveniently the bodies from slave infirmaries, medical school dispensaries, commercial hospitals, prisons, and plantation sick houses answered the call. Most slave owners allowed the deceased slave's body to be dissected by the attending doctor. If the slave had been executed his body automatically was procured for dissection. (20)

CHAPTER 5
MEDICAL EXPERIMENTATION

Medical and non-medical persons throughout the ages practiced medical experimentation. There were no restrictions on experimenting on what and by whom in America. The side effects, pain levels, and outcomes were not often known. It was a guessing game for many doctors and a fearful experience for the recipients. The slaves were not asked for their consent in many instances.

Today, America's medical community practices under very strict regulatory guidelines to perform investigative medical research. They are required to submit extensive supporting paperwork delineating who, what, where, expected outcomes, and possible side effects. Other requirements include description of subjects, financial concerns, benefits, disadvantages, contraindications, and consent forms. The research facility, hospital research committees and boards, and a Federal regulatory agency in certain cases must approve all of these items.

One of the most famous research doctors in the early 19th century was Dr. James Marion Sims of Montgomery, Alabama. He later became the Father of American Gynecology. His eight-bed infirmary was located behind his Perry Street office in Montgomery, Alabama. The second floor was used for surgical Negro cases. According to his autobiography, Sims "performed some of the most dangerous, yet personally and professionally significant, of his surgical operations." (21) His reputation of attending to hopeless and risky cases brought owners whose slaves had chronic problems for last-ditch efforts.

Sims' fame resulted in extensive surgical operations on slave women who, after delivery, developed vesico-vagina fistulas. This fistula is a tear between the vagina and bladder and results in urine dripping into the vagina, pain, and possible infection. For four years, Sims repeatedly performed unsuccessful operations on the same two slave women. He achieved success when he utilized silver sutures during one of the operations. Sims chose not to use anesthetics during the surgeries, erroneously believing that black women felt no pain and thus needed no anesthesia. (22) This was another aspect of Negro medicine that theorized Africans experience less pain during procedures than the white race.

Dr. Sims became famous throughout the medical world here and abroad for his discovery. The treatment of his subjects would be highly disapproved of today and no doubt would have difficulty obtaining research board approval. Sims' experiments paved the road for gynecological surgical discoveries.

Another Southern surgeon whose experiments cause us alarm was Dr. Thomas Hamilton of Jones County, Georgia. Dr. Hamilton performed agonizing experiments on a slave named John Brown, who was on loan from another planter. Hamilton was searching to find a treatment for sunstroke, a very common occurrence in the South. He tested various medications to determine if any drug could prevent or treat sunstroke.

In the slave's own words:

> The doctor ordered a hole to be dug in the ground, three feet and a half deep by three feet long, and two feet and a half wide. Into this pit, a quantity of dried oak bark was cast, and fire set to it. It was allowed to burn until the pit became heated like an oven, then the embers were taken out. A plank was then put across the bottom of the pit, and on that stool, having tested with a thermometer the degree which the pit was heated, the doctor bade me strip and get in, which I did only my head being above the ground. He then gave me some medicine, which he had prepared, and as soon as I was on the stool, a number of wet blankets were fastened over the hole, and scantlings (pieces of timber and cross sections) lay across them. This was to keep in the heat. It soon began to tell upon me; but though I tried hard to keep up against its effects, in

about half an hour I fainted. I was then lifted out and
revived, the doctor taking a note of the degree of heat
when I left the pit. (23)

According to Dr. Hamilton, his experiment found that cayenne
pepper tea accomplished the desired outcome. Hamilton marketed
his discovery and became quite wealthy. He also performed another
painful experiment on Brown to determine the thickness of the slave's
skin. These experiments lasted for nine months and left the slave
chronically debilitated. Brown survived to tell his story after escaping
to freedom.

CHAPTER 6
PLANTATION MEDICINE

The most widespread element of the African healthcare system was present on Southern plantations. Untrained owners and mistresses provided medical care to their own slaves. Many times Southern doctors gave directions to the owners, but there were just as many who found treatments in printed "recipe books" written for plantation owners and overseers to follow. Plantations were crude factories, isolated, and raised almost everything they needed. They also provided for the health of the family and the slaves. It should come as no surprise that slave owners wanted to keep their workers healthy, since the success of the plantation rode on the back of the workforce. Beating and starving the slaves would not be wise, since crippling would prevent them from doing their tasks. This was not true of cruel owners who punished slaves mercilessly.

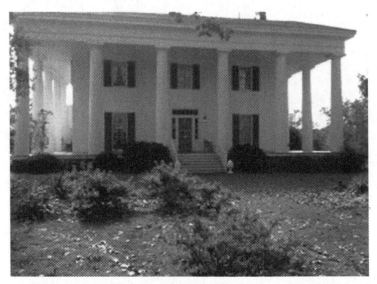

Barrington Hall circa 1842 Roswell, Georgia. Barrington Hall was not a crop-producing plantation but belonged to Barrington King, President of Roswell mill. Author's photo.

Indigo, rice, cotton, and sugar cane plantations could only be successful if there was an extensive healthy, young workforce performing the planting and harvesting. The plantation demanded a strict time schedule for these crucial activities. The owner could not afford for the slaves to be lying ill or injured in their cabins. Slave owners of antebellum America were very concerned and worried about the health of their slaves, who represented a sizable investment. The owner, his wife, and overseer paid a great deal of attention to the slave's medical complaints and provided rest and medical care as was required. If the slave seemed seriously ill, and the local home remedy did not work, a doctor was summoned to treat the slave. Doctors were contracted as fee-for-service or on an annual flat fee basis. (24)

Preventatively, doctors would weekly examine the slaves for fever, pleurisy, bowel complaints, flux, spasms, diseased legs, and abdominal pain. The elderly slaves whose job was to nurse in the sick houses secretly relied on their own African herbal remedies, much to the dismay of the white doctor (secrecy was paramount). The accepted "white" treatment of the day involved bleeding, puking, and purging for most complaints, which both slave owners and doctors employed. The majority of plantation owners and rural doctors were ignorant of the Negro medicine theories and practices that limited the use of the usual treatments. Slaves were hesitant to submit to the white man's treatments rather than use their own home remedies. The Africans trusted in their own Negro doctors and nurses who used African herbs and spells.

Many sugar planters in Louisiana and Mississippi also distrusted the white rural doctors because of the poor quality of care and the inability to stop the spread of infections. The planters preferred to treat medical cases themselves.

> During a cholera epidemic, Eli Landy, a sugar planter, administered laudanum, brandy, and frictions of cayenne to the bonds man. After consuming this heady and spicy brew Henry, the slave, died within six hours. (25)

The planter's self-help caused death, disability, and pain for the slave he treated.

Colonial and antebellum plantation owners were known to participate in the actual practice of medicine and experimentation on their slaves. President Thomas Jefferson, while residing in the White House, heard about a new method of inoculation against smallpox. Jefferson journeyed to Monticello to personally vaccinate his two hundred slaves against smallpox. (26)

Many planters filled their medicine chests with the latest cures that money could buy . . . quinine, sulfur, calomel, camphor, ipecac, and cream of tartar were favorites. Having the tools without the knowledge did not guarantee a cure. The distrust of white medicine led slaves to purposely not inform the owner or overseer when illness did occur, fearing the treatments that would surely be given. This attitude hampered the African healthcare system but probably saved more slave lives in the long term.

The slave owners delegated medical oversight of the plantation to the plantation mistress. She directed the medical care rendered to the ill or injured slave. The mistress ordered special foods for the ill and gave directions to the overseer. She "kept an eye on the management of the nursery where the babies of slave mothers who worked in the fields were kept between nursings." (27) The babies were future workers to add to the plantation's workforce and successful investments.

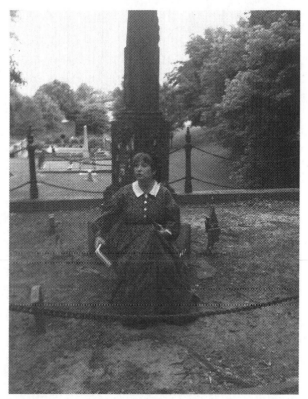

**Author portraying plantation mistress, Mrs. Henry
Dunwody at Confederate Major Dunwody's grave during
Roswell Historical Society's "Beyond The Stones" 2013**

According to Catherine Clinton, the plantation mistress often had
to assume responsibility as the ministering doctor and housekeeper.
Although older slave women were the actual nurses and attendants to
the sick, the mistress made daily rounds to the sick, invalid, and infant
community.

> They doctored the slaves both as humane plantation
> mistresses, seeing to the needs of their black charges
> and in their capacity as slave owners' wives, looking
> out for their husbands' property interests. (28)

These women kept "recipe books" with cures and remedies along with common cookbook items. They gave instructions what to do if complications occurred, listed remedies for poisonings and cures for opium overdoses. These non-medical women administered laudanum so freely that they kept recorded lists of prescribed minuscule dosages of the drug when given to infants. Laudanum is an alcoholic-based preparation with ten percent opium content. The mistress' training, if any, to dispense drugs and care for slaves and family probably occurred by watching and assisting her own mother as mistress of the home plantation.

Throughout the year, these women had to keep alert for signs of more serious disease such as smallpox. Although most slaves were inoculated on the large plantations, the vaccines sometimes failed especially among the children. At St. Simon's Island Retreat plantation, the mistress' nursing vigilance never ended.

> Of primary concern to Anna as a wife, mother, and plantation mistress was the health of those under her care at Retreat. She wrote constantly of the state of health of her husband, children, guests, and bond people. She asked constantly for reports of the health of absent family members and offered advice and sometimes preventatives and cures for the health risks associated with traveling to towns and cities north and south. (29)

The overseer was charged with managing the slave's health through instructions given from the owner or the mistress. If the overseer could read, he was given medical manuals to reference for signs and treatment of illnesses and injuries. Based upon his experience and the book's guidelines, the overseer chose the diet, medicines, and procedures to follow. All of the medicines would be recorded in a prescription book. (30) It seems so absurd that a foreman held the health and well being of hundreds of slaves in his hands. A few overseers had no medical guidance from the owner or his wife. Many of these men had no medical training and were often suspicious that slaves were malingering in order to get out of work or be given more and better food.

Some planters had very strict rules written for the overseer and the nursing attendants. One rice planter in South Carolina on the Pee Dee River instructed the overseer how to care for the sick slave:

> All sick persons are to stay in the hospital day and night, from the time the first complaint to the time they are able to go to work again. The nurses are responsible for the sick not to leave the house, and for the cleanliness of the bedding, utensils etc. The nurses are never to be allowed to give any medicine without the order of the overseer or doctor . . . In all cases, if at all serious, the doctor is to be sent for and his orders are to be strictly attended to; no alteration is to be made in the treatment he directs. (31)

The sick house could be a prison-like environment. The slaves were unable to see their family and had no control over their own bodies. They were crowded together and exposed to contagious diseases transmitted by air or direct contact with those infected. The nurses were also exposed to disease on a daily basis and slept in the sick house with their patients. Slaves became nurses if they were too old to work in the fields. They must be able to follow orders, be intelligent, be able to care for infants, and learn from the mistress' teachings and instructions.

The food for the sick slave was under the nurse's charge. Dr. Waring states that the aged and infirm were well cared for on the South Carolina rice plantations. Cherished family servants received extra consideration and attention regardless of the cost to the owner. (32) There are many first person post-war slave accounts that reinforced Waring's findings throughout the South.

Most large plantation sick houses were located at one end of the slave quarters, though not too close to risk contagion for the rest of the plantation populace. Visiting white doctors addressed the medical complaints from the slaves at the sick houses. There were many different designs of sick houses in Georgia. The facility could be one of the slave dwellings set aside for the ill or a large building with multiple levels.

The most elaborate slave sick houses were located on the Hopeton rice and sugar cane plantation of James Hamilton Couper and Cannon's Point, owned by John Couper, James' father. Each sick house was eighty feet by twenty-four feet with all the amenities. (33) They were described as airy and warm with four wards and an examining room, a medicine closet, a kitchen, and a bathing room. They were heated with steam and each person had a straw mattress on a cot with two blankets. The bedstraw was changed monthly and blankets washed then too. The wards were swept daily and washed out once a week. (34) The description gives an impression of a somewhat hygienic environment in which conscientious care was given; however, diseases still killed many slaves and residents of many plantations.

In 1828, Roswell King Jr., overseer of Pierce Butler's Georgia Rice Plantation on Butler Island, wrote in an agricultural journal:

> A hospital should be on each plantation, with proper
> nurses and apartments for lying—in women, for men
> and for a nursery; when any enter, they are not to
> leave the house until discharged. (35)

Butler's Hampton Plantation on ST. Simon Island had a large Negro sick house. The hospital building's structure was two and one-half stories high with four rooms and a loft; it was located at the end of the row of slave houses on the street (36)

**Remains of Butler Island rice plantation fields
outside Darien, GA, author's photo.**

Ruins of a sick house remain on St Simon's Island at Thomas Butler
King's Retreat plantation. The sick house mimicked those found at
Hopeton and Cannon Point. Made of tabby concrete, it was once
two and one-half stories tall with eight rooms, a large attic where the
nurses slept, and was heated by an internal fireplace. It was built to
care for three hundred slaves with its two rooms measuring fifteen by
twenty feet with windows. The sick house was larger than Retreat's
family mansion home, and was connected to the mansion house by a
rose-bordered walk that meandered through an orange grove. Today
it is a ruin with golf courses and a resort on the plantation grounds.
Thomas Butler King's Retreat is owned by the Sea Island Club. (37)

Pierce Butler allowed his slaves to farm their own small garden plot
and hunt wildlife to supplement their diets on St. Simon's Island.
These amenities became main stays in the African slave's diet.
Remains of the slaves' farming and hunting wastes were documented
through an archaeological excavation study of St. Anne's slave

settlement, part of the Butler plantations, by Brockington and Associates Inc. of Atlanta in 2005. (38)

Records indicate after the demise of the overseer, Roswell King Jr., a Dr. Wilson assumed the role from 1848-1860 at Hampton Plantation, the Butler cotton plantation on St. Simons. If Dr. Wilson practiced Negro medicine, then the St. Simon's Slaves were given specialized and often better medical treatment than the surrounding white population. I am unable at this time to confirm exactly what type of care he rendered but it certainly would be of value for future study.

Retreat Plantation Sick House exterior view, author's photo.

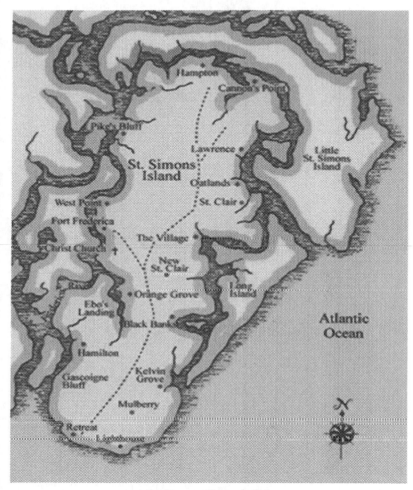

St. Simons Island, GA

Conclusion

Slave owners were motivated to protect their investment and property. Historical evidence supports that most slaves received good medical care, which was better than what the free colored and poor white Southern populations received pre-Civil War. It was all part of the African slave healthcare system. The slave owner had the monetary resources to acquire ample food, clothing, and housing for the slave, and he routinely hired medical doctors to treat the injured and ill. Personal diaries of plantation mistresses and planters tell stories of lives intertwined with their servants, the African slaves. These records add to our understanding of how and why the South felt compelled to provide medical care to an enslaved race.

PART 6 . . .

Basics of Negro Medicine

A little learning, indeed, may be a dangerous thing,
but the want of learning is a calamity to any people.
Frederick Douglass

Southern doctors of the early 19th century were adamant that the South had medical peculiarities only found within this region of America. This premise was based on the presence of Southern diseases, Southern climate, diet preferences, and a large African population. As a result, Negro medicine developed into a new medical specialty in the South, which primarily restricted the accepted European methods of treatment and drugs of the day.

The doctors, who specialized in this form of medicine, made a career in treating the African slaves and performing investigative studies. They published their studies in professional texts and articles to share with medical peers and slave owners. Negro medicine made it possible for the doctor to remain economically sound and demonstrate his clinical skills. His clientele were readily available and sufficient in numbers to support the Negro specialist. The slave owner paid the physician to provide preventative and acute medical care to the plantation African population. The plantation or slave owner would thus be ensured of a healthy work force. (1, 2)

Chapter 1
NEGRO MEDICINE'S THEORIES

Physician-scientists

The African was exposed to a harsh and hot environment; he was poorly clothed and given less than a nutritious diet. Slaves who were exhausted or had anemia could not tolerate the white man's blood volume depletion procedures. These observations were known even during Thomas Jefferson's time when he simply recorded, "Never bleed a Negro." Few doctors took note of these findings until a select group of Southern antebellum doctors theorized and experimented with this new medical specialty. (3)

These doctors theorized that medically, the African's body could not tolerate the dramatic decrease of blood volume and dehydration from bleeding and the caustic drugs. This proposition was based on the physiological differences between the Africans and the European white race. Negro medicine grew upon this racial foundation, which supported in their minds the inferiority of the African race and slavery. The most renowned of these physician/scientists were Doctors Nott, Merrill, Yandell, Wilson, Cartwright, and Tidyman.

Bloodletting and Other Depletion Techniques

Dr. John Steinbach Wilson of Columbus, Georgia, was one of several Southern doctors who cautioned about depleting bodily fluids in Africans. Others such as Dr. Josiah Clark Nott and Dr. Samuel A. Cartwright agreed with Wilson's conclusions. Dr. Wilson had plans to publish a textbook on Negro health and medicine but because of the outbreak of the Civil War, the printing never occurred. Interestingly, it was not until 1975 that the first medical history textbook on Negroes was published and written by an African American physician. (4)

Dr. Tidyman, a planter from South Carolina, also observed and proposed that the urban African required less bleeding than whites. He saw that the black race had less vital resistance than whites.

Dr. Cartwright developed more extensive theories about Negro health and medicine. He was in agreement with those who advised against the indiscriminate use of bloodletting and caustic drugs on the African. His advice was rather to treat the Negro by guarding him from the open air, keeping him out of the sun, and restricting him to a light diet of tea and soup. This would cause the disease merely to run its dreadful course. (5)

Ironically, it was a highly respected Philadelphian, Dr. Nathaniel Chapman, who was the first to officially caution the medical community about bloodletting the African race. Few doctors would give up this practice however and many did not stop until the African lost consciousness.

Periodic and Intermittent Fevers

Dr. A. P. Merrill of Memphis, Tennessee, and Dr. Josiah Nott of Mobile, Alabama, recognized that certain slaves in specific regions of the South had immunity against contracting periodic fevers. These fevers are known as malaria in early 20th century. Nott documented that other slaves, especially on Carolina coastal rice plantations, were able to develop periodic fevers or were born with resistance to them. Merrill noted this same phenomena occurring in the lower Mississippi Valley plantations. Nott saw that there were "two different types of marsh fever, one found in the lowlands and the other in hilly interiors. (6)

Dr. Philip Tidyman also wrote about fevers among the Africans in the *Philadelphia Journal of Medicine*. He observed Africans with certain fevers, found in areas of stagnant water on rice plantations, were easily treated with cold-water baths. These same fevers were disastrous to the white population within the same geographical area. This particular fever did not return to the previously treated African. Most white doctors recommended cold-water baths for fever-stricken whites but not for the Africans. (7)

Intelligence and Racial Inferiority

By 1848, Dr. Samuel A. Cartwright of New Orleans became famous by publishing his articles on Negro medicine in Southern journals. He became chair of Louisiana's Medical Association and the committee to investigate black health and physiology. In one of his papers, he suggested that because of the African's physical and mental defects, it was nearly impossible for the slave to survive without the white man's care and supervision. He described the cranium of Africans to be ten percent smaller than whites; therefore, the brain was unable to develop intellectually. He further surmised that the African's odd-shaped head held an inferior brain. He stated that this was demonstrated with the behavior of laziness and lack of desire to care for himself. (8)

Dr. Cartwright also postulated that dysentery, colic, and other illnesses were born from the African's state of the mind. Therefore, no white man's treatments could cure the African; that superstition was the genuine cause of the high mortality in Africans.

Dr. Merrill's investigations added more substance for racial inferiority. His findings showed that the African race's peculiarities required a different treatment and severity from those given to the white population. He conceded that it would take many thousands of years for the African to evolve into the present white man's state. (9) This certainly supported the proslavery mentality of the South, giving credence to their stance.

Heat and Cold

Dr. Merrill believed that the African was very susceptible to cold climates as a result of his dark-colored skin and heritage of a hot African climate. His medical treatment of the slaves was based on this idea. Merrill's advice to slave owners was to provide warm clothing and appropriate shelter during cold weather. Dr. Cartwright theorized that there was a physiological difference in the African race, which required a slave to cover his head with a blanket while sleeping. As a result, the African would inhale warm, moist air thus able to survive the cold climate. Overall, the African endured heat better than whites because of his thicker skin and wooly head of hair. These traits made the African slave ideal for working in the South's hot climate.

Respiratory Diseases

The African was more susceptible to contracting a cold and other respiratory diseases. Dr. Daniel Drake of the Mississippi Valley affirmed that inflammation of the lungs, or pneumonia, and other respiratory illnesses were devastating to Africans. Dr. Cartwright claimed that the Negro's lungs functioned inefficiently and this made Africans susceptible to all types of respiratory illnesses found in America.

In 1831, Dr. Lunsford Yandell from Nashville, Tennessee, performed autopsies on five Africans diagnosed with Negro poison also called Negro consumption. He studied the disease, which he named Struma Africana, a fatal yet common illness found among slaves. This disease's symptomatology included fever, enlarged lymph glands, spleen, and liver, diarrhea, shortness of breath, and general body wasting. His autopsies revealed tubercles and pneumonia in the lungs. These findings were different than the white man's consumption or tuberculosis. Today this disease has been recognized as miliary or extra pulmonary tuberculosis, a highly deadly and contagious form of tuberculosis. (10)

Another type of tuberculosis observed in both Africans and whites was called scrofula, which was characterized by large swelling of the neck lymph glands, and generalized wasting away until death. Yandell noted the African skin became pale and dry, lips and nose protruded, and eye corneas turned a bluish cast. As the scrofula TB progressed, the heartbeat grew faster and difficulty breathing increased. The African's fever was never very high but the neck lymph glands became enormous in size. Yandell's recommendation was to prevent the disease through cleanliness and improved ventilation and decreased crowding in the African's environment. This form of tuberculosis is now known as pulmonary tuberculosis involving the scrofula lymph glands. (11)

Dirt Eating

Cachexia Africana, or dirt eating, was considered peculiar to only the African race. Dr. W. M. Carpenter researched this habit and declared only the colored possessed this disease. All African tribes indulged in eating large amounts of clay as a social habit. West Indies doctors supported that the African used dirt eating as a method to commit suicide. As a result of these studies, Southern doctors declared African dirt eating was caused by a mental impairment. They thought African children developed this habit as a result of improper and prolonged lactation. Such children exhibited the potbelly stomach distention. (12, 13) Dr. Cartwright felt dirt eating could be cured because it was due to a state of the mind. He proposed that African counter charm, a native African treatment, would overcome the mental impression and superstitions.

Other Unacceptable Behaviors

Cartwright also wrote extensively on African behavior caused by mental impairment. He designated two well-known behaviors in the South as *Drapetomania* and *Dysaethesia Aethiopica*. These Greek terms he created were very impressive to the Southern medical profession and widely published by Cartwright. *Drapetomania* caused the African to run away from his master to obtain his freedom. *Dysaethesia Aethiopica* or "rascality" described the state where the African did mischief by breaking items, stealing, being careless with property belonging to others, and also the inability to stay alert and awake. Cartwright reinforced the stance that only Southern doctors who were trained in and practiced Negro medicine could adequately treat the African maladies. (14)

High Infant Mortality

Throughout the South, there were two major conditions that caused a high slave infant mortality. It was widely accepted that they did not exist within the white population, probably because of under reporting by embarrassed white parents.

Neonatal African infant slaves were at risk to experience an onset of convulsions and death. This phenomenon occurred seven to ten days after delivery. At first the infant refused to nurse breast milk and then rigidity of fists, feet, entire muscular system, and bending back of the head soon set in. These symptoms progressed to suffocation and death by about day eighteen.

The other condition was called smothering or overlaying. It generally occurred from two weeks to four months of age. Physicians and slave owners felt that the exhausted slave mother rolled on the infant when she slept resulting in the suffocation of the child.

Documentation of such a case in Savitt reveals that the child had previously had a mild nasal discharge but was in excellent health. Although the infant was placed face down in the crib with the head turned to the side, the baby was found dead in the morning. (15)

Southern doctors summarized the basic characteristics of slave health.

> Infant mortality was much more prevalent among blacks than whites (2:1) . . . although the former had greater longevity once childhood was survived; blacks were less susceptible to intermittent fever or malaria; blacks were more susceptible to respiratory disease and to disease associated with cold weather; blacks had more dental disease; black women were naturally more adept at easy childbirth . . . (16)

CHAPTER 2
MODERN MEDICAL RESEARCH AND FINDINGS

Recognizing that the African healthcare system existed throughout the Old South, I came to wonder if any of the theories and treatments were actually valid. I decided to investigate each of the accepted theories that were basic to Negro medicine. I found that some of those theories were supported by modern scientific research, while others had no evidence and was based solely on racial prejudice.

The following are the seven Negro medicine theories I examined: bloodletting and other depletion techniques, periodic and intermittent fevers, intelligence and racial inferiority, heat and cold, respiratory disease, dirt eating, other unacceptable behaviors, and high infant mortality.

Theory #1 Bloodletting and other depletion techniques

Bloodletting was quite prevalent during the 18th century but it eventually decreased by the Civil War. Depletion theory began with the Greeks who discovered the inflammatory theory. The Greeks removed volumes of blood from the body along with poisonous waste products to eliminate the irritant that caused disease. Following the Greek practice, antebellum doctors removed one quart of the blood at most. On average, the human body contains five to six quarts of blood. (17)

Frequent bloodletting resulted in further stress on the body in people with iron depleted diets, diseased states, fever, and injuries. Severe loss of blood volume also decreased the number of red blood cells, which carry oxygen, and white blood cells that protect the body against infection and tissue injury. It also decreases the number of platelets required during the normal clotting process. As a result of these processes, cell metabolism is affected with buildup of waste products that remain in cells causing poor functioning and death of the tissue.

Decreased oxygen levels to the vital organs of the brain, heart, lungs, and liver results in heart failure and low blood pressure, eventually leading to shock.

A state of shock exists when the heart pumps blood inadequately. It can also occur when there is excessive dilation of the body's blood vessels. Cell damage follows and shock quickly becomes irreversible. Symptoms of shock are sleepiness, confusion, cold, and sweaty skin, appearing pale or bluish in tone. (18)

When the physician removed the blood of injured soldiers, the risk of death increased dramatically. As doctors became more experienced in traumatic battlefield medicine, they realized they had to change their clinical approach to care to save lives. Prior to this time, most populations were still receiving this deadly therapy.

Dr. Cartwright's advice in caring for the Negro revealed the soundest approach by improving the Negro diet, providing for rest, ensuring a clean environment, and lessening exposure to the elements. If his advice worked for the Negro slaves, it certainly would have been good for white soldiers. To us today, these guidelines seem like common-sense health measures. Who hasn't heard from a physician to rest, eat a healthy diet, and stay away from others who have infectious diseases, especially during the flu season? (19)

Dr. Tidyman's recognition that the black race has less vital resistance is also true. He missed the point of what caused the decreased resistance to disease. As a result of severe working conditions, lack of rest, poor diet with few vegetables and even less protein, the Negro lost much of his immunity to diseases. Most slaves experienced some form of anemia, pellagra, and scurvy because of their meager diet. The lack of iron, vitamins, and minerals led to disease; when sickness was treated with depletion therapy, the slave quickly became debilitated. (20) Most Southern slaves' diet consisted of corn, molasses, and a small amount of meat at Christmas and other infrequent celebrations. If the master permitted, the slave could add to their diet by growing their own vegetables on a small plot of land near the slave cabins.

Theory #2 Periodic or Intermittent Fevers

Doctors described fevers as malaria, which flourished in the Southern coastal lands. The term "fever" represented many diseases such as swamp fever, country fever, summer fever, bilious fever, and broken bone fever, remittent, intermittent and recurring fevers instead of diseases, as we know them today. (21)

Malaria

Malaria is an infection within the red blood cells (RBC's) as a result of a bite from a female Anopheles mosquito. The culprit is a single-celled organism (parasite), the Plasmodium (P). There are four species of this parasite that infect humans: *P. vivax, P. ovale, P. falciparum and P. malariae.* The malarial parasitic life cycle begins when a female mosquito bites a human who has malaria. The mosquito ingests the human blood that contains the parasite, which moves immediately to the mosquito's salivary glands. As the mosquito bites a new human, the parasite is then injected, mixed in its saliva, into the human's blood stream. The parasite floats to the liver and begins to multiply. It takes two to four weeks for the parasite to mature and invade the RBC's of the human. Once in the RBC, the parasite multiplies again until the RBC ruptures.

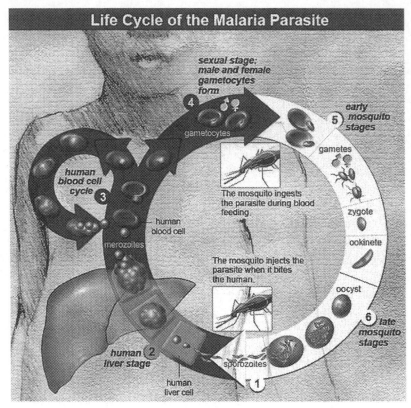

Courtesy of NIAID http://ww.niaid.nih.gov

Each of the four parasitic species causes intermittent or repeated attacks of the malarial symptoms. Mild jaundice with an enlarged spleen and liver, chills, and fever are common with all forms of malaria. The most deadly and severe form is the *P. falciparum*, which can result in abnormal brain function, black water fever, and rupture of RBC's released into the urine. *P. falciparum and P. vivax* malarias are the most common forms found in North America. The *vivax* form is generally located farther from the coast within the interior and piedmont country and can affect victims for many years. (22) Dr. Nott was correct when he proposed that there were two different swamp fevers and their locations differ, one if found on the coast and the other within the interior.

The Negro médicine doctors suggested only the African could be immune to intermittent fever. This notion is false: any person who was raised in an area where malaria was prevalent and survived repeated infections, would acquire a level of immunity. They would not be acutely ill and did not die from that form of malaria, but were chronically ill.

There are race-specific immunities to malaria. African Americans in the 21st century who lack the Duffy antigen are immune from the *P. vivax*. This antigen prevents the parasite from penetrating the RBC. Savitt references medical research that ninety percent of West Africans and seventy percent African Americans lack Duffy antigens. Since the *P. vivax* requires the Duffy-positive RBC, the Negro slaves and free blacks from West Africa were immune to the *vivax* form of malaria. (23)

Protection against the most malignant form of malaria *(P. Falciparum)* came from an abnormal sickling gene of the sickle cell disease and sickle cell trait. Sickle cell disease is an inherited condition that is characterized by RBC's that have a sickle-like shape and develop a chronic hemolytic anemia. This gene is inherited from West African and Sub-Sahara tribes affecting ten percent of African Americans in the United States. If the person has one sickle cell gene they will have the sickle cell trait. He will not develop the full-blown sickle cell disease, but is a mere carrier. If he has two sickle cell genes, he will develop sickle cell disease. With the disease, the RBC's have an abnormal type of hemoglobin that reduces the amount of oxygen carried to the body's tissues. The cells become crescent in shape and blocks smaller blood vessels within the body's organs. The result is reduced oxygen and severe sickle cell anemia from the breakdown of the fragile RBC's. Decreased oxygen also depletes cells of potassium and kills the malaria parasite located in the cell.

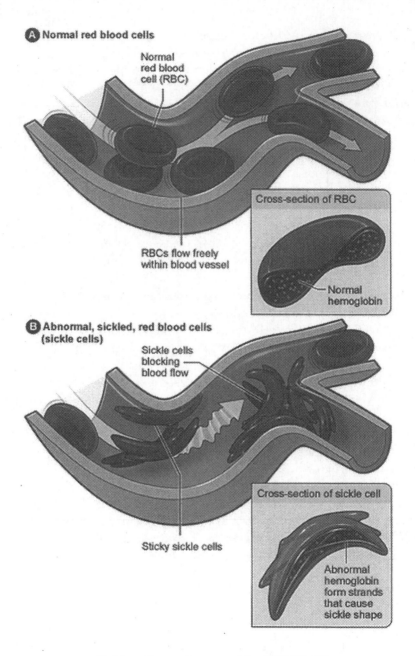

Sickle cell anemia granted by NHLBI, US
Dept. of Health and Human Services

Those victims of sickle cell disease develop enlarged spleens as children. As the child grows into adulthood, the spleen shrinks and is no longer able to help the body fight infection. Anemia becomes severe with heart enlargement. Heart murmurs, fever, and bone and joint pain were common. Hip joints were often severely damaged resulting in the slave developing mobility limitations. A sickle cell crisis in adults occurred from hypoxic death of tissue as blood flow became blocked. In the past, people with sickle cell disease barely lived beyond twenty years of age.

Today, young African American females with sickle cell disease or sickle cell anemia have a high rate of miscarriage. This is probably the same reason for the high rate of miscarriages of young African female slaves in the 18th and 19th centuries. It may also be responsible for the high mortality rate of slave children who died before reaching twenty years of age. Sickle cell anemia increases the Negro's sensitivity to lung infections, especially pneumococcal pneumonia. The slave with sickle cell disease experienced joint pain and was diagnosed as rheumatism in the Old South. (24,25,26)

Another genetic condition that rendered some immunity to malaria is G-6-PD (glucose 6 phosphate dehydrogenase) deficiency. Researchers found a sex-linked gene with a high incidence in the slave trading ports of Africa. Today the gene is present in ten percent of African Americans.

Yellow Fever

Yellow Fever is classified as an arbovirus infection caused by a virus that spreads to humans through insect bites. Biting contagious animals infected these insects. Yellow fever is the most historical arbovirus infection man has known; it has been around for a long time. Once infected, it causes fever, bleeding, and jaundice and is usually fatal. "The mosquito is the primary carrier between monkeys, from monkeys to humans, and from person to person." (27)

Specifically in Africa, the yellow fever occurs in small-scale epidemics. The mosquito bites humans and monkeys alike since they both breed around human dwellings. Humans can also contract the virus from eating infected monkey meat.

In urban areas of the South, larger epidemics have occurred when infected people came into densely populated areas of non-immune people or exposed to mosquito breeding grounds. We can understand why diseased ships entering colonial harbors were quarantined in the past. The port of antebellum Norfolk, Virginia, was the major point of entry for yellow fever epidemics. The disease remained within the city proper and did not spread into the countryside. The ports of Portsmouth and Alexandria also suffered from yellow fever epidemics.

Dr. Tidyman's observation concerning stagnant water having an impact on fever was partially correct. He had no knowledge that this type of water was the breeding ground for the disease-carrying mosquito for both malaria and yellow fever.

The Africans did not contract yellow fever as often as whites and if they did become infected, the case was milder. Generations of Africans have been repeatedly exposed to yellow fever in Africa resulting in an acquired immunity, but the early white American settlers had never experienced this illness. Tropical research today records that even West African descendants have the defense mechanism for this illness. They have less severe cases of yellow fever and never are fatal. (28)

Modern medical science doesn't have a clear reason for the yellow fever immunity mechanism of the African American today. Scientists concur that the Negro medicine experts of the Old South were correct that the African possessed a resistance to yellow fever.

Theory #3 Intelligence and Racial Inferiority

Drs. Cartwright and Merrill were two of the many Southern doctors who attempted to provide sound "scientific" data to support the African's inferiority to the white man. Today's science examines the connection between race and intelligence theory using the intelligence quotient (IQ), developed in the 20th century. Studies within scientific communities including psychology, anthropology, biology, and sociology discuss the relationship between IQ and the races. I will briefly relate a few.

There's a significant variation between racial groups on IQ tests in the United States. Overall, African ancestry has lower IQ scores than European ancestry, while East Asian ancestry is higher than the European scores. Causes for these differences in scores are examined within four classifications. The first premise can be found in group intelligence itself, as a result of environmental factors and inherited differences in brain function. The second lies in cognitive ability caused by social or environmental factors. The third stance states there are no differences in races but differences lie in the inappropriateness of the tests. The fourth claims comparison between races means nothing because of the vagueness and poorly constructed concepts of the terms race and intelligence.

The American Psychological Association finds that no adequate explanation for the racial IQ gap is presently available. The American Anthropological Association's position is that intelligence can't be biologically determined by race. Interestingly, the American Association of Physical Anthropologists affirms:

> It (intelligence) does not affect the ability of a population to function in any social setting, all peoples possess equal biological ability to assimilate any human culture and racist political doctrines find no foundation in scientific knowledge concerning modern or past human populations. (29)

Alan Templeton argues that racial groups neither represent sub-species or distinct evolutionary lineages and that, therefore, there is no basis for making claims about the general intelligence of races. (30) Further researchers Beal and Lieberman conclude that even though there may be variation in brain size, the variation should be examined based on biogeographic ancestry and separate from race. Lastly, Cernovsky, in 1997, concluded that a difference in average brain size varies from country to country. The average brain size of the Maasai African is larger than that of the average Caucasoid Egyptian. (31, 32)

To further disclaim the inferiority of the African slave race, individual achievements of the African American's ability to survive and his degree of cognitive function is witnessed by the awarding of the Nobel Prize. There have been black recipients in three of the six award categories: economy, peace, and literature. Out of the eight hundred individual recipients, fifteen have been of a black race. (33)

The *Journal of Blacks in Higher Education* publishes a chronological list of African Americans who accomplished noteworthy feats. I have chosen a few listed who lived before, during, or after the Civil war: (34)

Prior to the Civil War, some blacks were educated in institutions of higher learning. In 1804, Middlebury College awards an honorary master's degree to Lemuel Haynes, a black person who fought in the Revolutionary War. By 1823, Alexander Lucius Twilight becomes the first known black person to graduate from a college in the United States. Edward Jones graduates in 1826 from Amherst College and is believed to be the second black person to earn a college degree. James McCune Smith, in 1837, is the first black person to earn a medical degree when he graduated from the University of Glasgow in Scotland. Smith returned to the U.S. to be a physician. In 1847, David J. Peck is the first black person to earn a degree from a medical college in the United States at Rush Medical College in Chicago. In 1862, Mary Jane Patterson, a teacher, graduates with a bachelor's degree from Oberlin College as the first black woman to earn a bachelor's degree.

Forty blacks had already graduated from Northern colleges by the end of the Civil War. In 1869, George Lewis Ruffin is the first black person to earn a degree from Harvard Law School, and became Massachusetts' first African American judge. Patrick Francis Healy, a former slave who passed for white, is named president of Georgetown University in 1874. He was the first black person at a predominantly white higher-education institution in the United States. In 1881, Tuskegee Institute was established in Alabama with Booker T. Washington as its first principal. Robert Robinson Taylor was the first black person in 1892 to graduate from the Massachusetts Institute of Technology. Daniel Hale Williams, a graduate of Chicago Medical College (now Northwestern University Medical School), performed the world's first successful open heart surgery 1893.

Black people earned advanced degrees in many fields of sciences in the early twentieth century. ST. Elmo Brady becomes the first black person to earn a doctorate in chemistry in 1916, and his Ph.D. at the University of Illinois. Thomas Wyatt Turner is the first Black person awarded a Ph.D. in botany from Cornell University in 1921. Arnold Hamilton Maloney, the discoverer of the antidote for barbiturate poisoning, was the first black person to graduate with a Ph.D. in pharmacology from the University of Wisconsin in 1931. Also in 1931, Jane Matilda Bolin was the first black woman graduate of Yale Law School, and the nation's first black woman judge in 1939. Columbia University awards the first doctorate to a black person in bacteriology, Hildrus Augustus Poindexter, in 1932.

To summarize, the Negro physician/scientist and Southerners in general were wrong about the African's intelligence. Their legacies are the great achievements that encouraged future dreams for African Americans. Black Americans demonstrated a high degree of motivation and intelligence in the 19th and 20th centuries to succeed in reaching their goals.

Theory #4 Heat and Cold

Savitt references two studies in the 20th century that examined cold tolerance of the African American population during the Korean War. These findings reveal that African Americans adapt more poorly to cold exposure than whites. These major physiological changes occur:

> Their metabolic rates do not increase significantly until after (those of) whites and even then they do not rise as much. Their first shivers occur at a lower skin temperature than for whites and their incidence of frostbite is higher and their cases more severe than those of whites. (35)

There is sufficient scientific clinical data to support the Old South's observation that, indeed, the African slave was very susceptible to cold. Dr. Merrill was correct in providing appropriate clothing and shelter during cold weather.

Dr. Tidyman's treatment to reduce fever with cold-water applications remains foundational as a comfort measure and reduces fever. Modern medical research demonstrates that the body's mild fever is a sign that the immune system is at work. Higher temperatures will reset the hypothalamus of the brain and assist to fight the offending organism.

Hyperthermia, however, can be deadly when extreme temperature is associated with such conditions as heat stroke. This scenario requires immediate heat reducing measures with cold applications. The body is no longer able to control its thermostat. The 1850 mortality census supports the South's theory that, compared to slaves, whites are much more intolerant of heat. Heat stroke, a common deadly condition in the South, was studied in America and British West Indies. Observations revealed working slaves suffered less heat stroke than whites when both performed equally laborious tasks. Attempting to explain these phenomena, Savitt quotes Dr. John Von Errie in 1861, "The Negro's excretory system relieves him from all those climatic influences so fatal to the white populations." (36)

Modern medical science supports this premise as well. When studied, the African American and white populations have an inherent ability to release sodium, chloride, and other electrolytes through urine and sweat. The loss of these in large amounts results in heat prostration or heat stroke. The African American has the ability to release smaller amounts compared to the white race.

Further study by Strydom and Wyndam in 1963 discusses the physiological mechanism and acclimation to heat. Their conclusion was based on equal activity in same environments over time: both whites and blacks have little differences in heat tolerance.

Historically, the African slave quickly acclimated to the southern harsh climate and hard labor, more so than whites. The white 19th century Southern gentry were unaccustomed to hard physical outdoor activity and exposure to the hot weather. (37)

Theory #5 Respiratory Diseases

Tuberculosis (TB)

TB has been known since ancient times. Major epidemics attacked Europe in the overcrowded cities during the Industrial Revolution. The Europeans who survived developed a TB resistant gene and passed it to later generations. The African slaves had not been exposed to TB until they arrived in America. Their risk was very high to contract the disease. Even today, African Americans have had less time to develop TB resistant genes, and TB is more common in them than the whites.

TB is a contagious and highly fatal infection caused by the bacteria *Mycobacterium (M)*. This bacteria causes *(M) Tuberculosis, (M) Bovis, and (M) Africanum*. Two of the three forms of TB exist in humans: *(M) tuberculosis and (M) Africanum. (M) Bovis* exists in cattle. Active tuberculosis begins in the lungs; if it spreads to the blood stream, it will affect other parts of the body. This form is called extra-pulmonary tuberculosis. Extra-pulmonary TB includes lymphadenitis (scrofula), which was so widely recorded during the antebellum period. Pulmonary TB can be either primary or secondary in nature.

TB is acquired through several methods of transmission. *(M) Tuberculosis* is contracted in the air through suspended droplets. The *(M) Bovis* is acquired through unpasteurized milk infected with the organism. A fetus may acquire TB before or during the birth process by swallowing infected amniotic fluid or breathing infected air droplets during delivery. *(M) Africanum* is mostly found in West Africa but is also spread airborne from an infected person. This type of TB primarily affects those with active HIV. (38, 39)

The African slave contracted what Southerners called Struma Africana, or Negro consumption, which was probably miliary TB. In this highly contagious and fatal disease, the TB organism has entered the blood stream and resides in all of the body's organs. The African was placed at risk if debilitated from other diseases and harsh environmental factors. Malnourishment, exhaustion, and overcrowding also predisposed the slave to develop TB. (40) Their environment provided ideal conditions for TB to spread.

When Southern doctors reviewed their statistics and saw the high TB mortality rate among slaves, they surmised that the African was medically different from whites. Knowing now that the African possessed a much smaller TB resistant gene pool than European whites, we can agree that they were medically different because of lack of hereditary immunity and harsh environmental factors.

Pneumonia

Inflammation of the lungs or pneumonia was known to be deadly to the African race. The African slave was first exposed to bacterial pneumonias upon arriving in America. They were also less able to resist other respiratory infections as well. The Southern doctor declared that the African's physiology was to blame for their increased vulnerability to respiratory diseases.

There remains within the scientific medical community disagreement about the African American population's susceptibility to lung infections. Throughout the early 20th century, pulmonary infections were studied environmentally and anthropologically. Findings show that moving from a hot tropical climate to a milder climate decreases the African American's ability to fight off pneumonia-causing bacteria. They also confirmed their resistance decreases with exposure to cold and wet weather. Public health experts have observed that overcrowding and unsanitary environments resulted in increased numbers of respiratory diseases in African American and white poverty areas. The question remains unanswered. Did racial physiology or environmental conditions cause the high incidence of respiratory disease in the African slave and African Americans today? (41)

Theory #6 Dirt Eating and Other Unacceptable Behaviors

Cachexia Africana was a disorder where African slaves ate non-food substances such as dirt or clay. Today, this disorder is diagnosed as PICA. The cravings for unusual items are probably related to malnutrition or some religious or cultural aspect. Dirt eating was practiced in early civilizations and continues within various African and South American peoples. (42, 43)

Historically, the ancient Greek youth ingested clay to become slender. The Chinese were noted to mix gypsum with a jelly to eat daily. Historian James Maxwell notes that in Africa, women form clay into balls and sell them in market places, as a social practice. He further relates that during the slave trade days, groups of Negroes indulged in excessive dirt eating believing that after death they would return to their homeland. (44) He surmised that the African was seeking suicide.

Iron deficiency anemia may be the underlying cause for this strange craving disorder. As red blood cells (RBC's) are lost, large amounts of iron are also depleted. A diet low in iron may cause a deficiency in infants and children, which hampers their growth. In adults, anemia indicates a severe loss of blood, usually through gastrointestinal bleeding or menstrual bleeding in women. (45)

The slave's diet lacked iron producing meats and vegetables that accounts for the iron deficiency anemia.

Another cause of anemia is hemolysis or destruction of RBC's from an abnormality within the RBC from sickle cell anemia or G6PD deficiency.

Southern slave owners and doctors tried in vain to stop African Cachexia since it debilitated the working slave or caused his death. Dirt eating by slaves also aided the ingestion of contaminated soil containing worms and other parasites, resulting in serious diseases.

Clay pancakes sold in African markets, image credited to Ariana Cubillos of the Associated Press.

Theory #7 Other Unacceptable Behavior

Research is not necessary to disprove Dr. Cartwright's *Drapetomania* or *Dysaethesia Aethiopica*. The desire to be free is basic to all races of man. Acting upon this need, the African slave implemented the plan to be free by running away to escape from his master's control.

Passive-aggressive behavior was another means to be free and release anger through destroying property, stealing, faking illness, and avoidance of work. When the slave lost hope of ever being free, despondency and depression resulted, as seen in lack of a sanitary environment and personal grooming. Similar behaviors were exhibited by Native Americans when they were enslaved by the early colonists; many of these people refused to work and often died from unknown causes when their freedom was taken. Slavery of these native people would end when the ample supply of African slaves became available to Southern plantations.

Theory #8 High Infant Mortality

Sudden Infant Death Syndrome (SIDS)

While sickle cell anemia resulted in many miscarriages and infant deaths, other conditions identified in the 20th century may explain the slaves' high infant mortality. Smothering, overlaying, or suffocation were assumed causes of antebellum infant deaths. Today, these infant deaths are diagnosed as Sudden Infant Death Syndrome (SIDS). Modern research and clinical data clearly establishes that SIDS is a leading killer of infants two weeks to one year of age, although the prime target group is two weeks to four months. If there existed a difference between African slaves and whites, it would be explained by socioeconomic factors and not race.

SIDS is the unexpected sudden death of a healthy infant. It occurs more during winter months and in lower socioeconomic families. There is a higher incidence of SIDS among premature infants, in families whose siblings died of SIDS, and newborn infants who required resuscitation at birth. Additional research shows a higher risk for teenage mothers, mothers who smoke during pregnancy, and in male babies. (46, 47, 48)

Infants who sleep on their stomach and sleep on soft bedding are factors that may lead to SIDS. Some infants who experience mild respiratory or gastrointestinal infections were also diagnosed with SIDS. (49)

Tetanus

African slave neonatal infants who experienced convulsions and death by day eighteen died from Neonatal Tetanus. Clinical antebellum records support that the infant's umbilical cord stump became infected. Twentieth century science surmises that the infection was caused by *Clostridium Tetani (C) Tetani*. This is an anaerobic gram-positive spore former that lives in soil. (50)

Tetanus occurs today in poorly immunized non-white and elderly persons in the United States. The contamination with the *(C) Tetani* spore occurs after an acute injury like a puncture wound. The spores grow in tissue where there is lack of oxygen and produce a toxin that affects the motor neurons of the victim. Muscles become rigid and eventually cause paralysis and the victim stops breathing.

Tetanus was fatal prior to the 20th century. Immunizations to prevent tetanus are routinely given today. Those who are not immunized and exposed to tetanus receive antibiotics and human tetanus immune globulins. Drugs to control muscle spasms are also given. (51)

It's true the African slaves were more prone to tetanus because of the filthy living conditions. On some plantations, night wastes were deposited by slaves on the ground around the slave quarters. The planters had the contaminated soil gathered twice a year, which was distributed within the growing fields as manure. Here, the field hand slaves worked with bare feet and unprotected hands. These fields were worked by both sexes and at the end of the workday, female slaves still had to care for their infants. Sanitary measures were afterthoughts among the poor exhausted slave, as a result there was a very high risk of Neonatal Tetanus in the rural slave population. (52)

Neonatal infants' umbilical cord stumps were exposed to *(C) Tetani* and developed tetanus rapidly. Scientists agree the spores in the soil were transferred to the cords at or soon after birth.

Conclusion

There were definitely some diseases in the Old South whose infectiousness, prognosis, and treatment were different for African slaves than the European/Caucasians. Interpretations led to certain prejudices during the time of slavery. Southern doctors and slave owners used these differences to support the legitimacy of slavery and the Negro healthcare system.

There are racial differences in diseases and treatments recorded by American medical scientists. Genetic differences persist between the races as demonstrated through studies by the American Lung Association and other public health agencies. Seven deadly diseases affect the African American more so than the European-white American. These diseases are diabetes, asthma, sarcoidosis, lung cancer, hypertension, sudden infant death syndrome, heart disease, stroke, and sickle cell disease. The incidence is higher in the African American not only because of genetic disposition, but also because of environmental and socioeconomic factors. Health care disparities such as access to healthcare, attitudes of distrust, and economic issues add to the medical differences experienced by the African American. (53, 54)

PART 7

African Medicine of the 1800's

*Since new developments are the products of a creative
mind, we must therefore stimulate and encourage that
type of mind in every way possible.*
George Washington Carver

Overview

We have explored the many elements of the African slave healthcare
system. The last and probably the most influential were the traditions
brought from Africa, which the slaves utilized and had faith in to
heal their illnesses. This included self-help where slaves chose and
administered their own treatments. The other elements of the African
healthcare system have ceased to operate, but many of the traditional
African medicine and herbs continue to be useful in the 21st century
folk healings.

The leaves and roots of plants and tree bark have been used to treat
illness since ancient times. Oral traditions describe various cures
that may or may not have been effective. Those that proved deadly
or useless are lost to history. It was not until written history that
mankind recorded attempts to use nature to cure illness and relieve
suffering.

Some of the early cures included religious and spiritual components.
Superstition offered hope to those seeking remedies where none

existed. It should not surprise us that healing herbs, religious customs, and superstitions built the foundation of folk medicine.

There were two forms of folk medicine identified in America's recent past. Native Americans, European whites, and African descent peoples used both forms of folk medicine. The first, natural or herbal folk medicines, were based on plants, herbs, minerals and animal components. The second, magico-religious, or occult folk medicine, worked with charms, actions, and suggestive language to produce cures. (1)

CHAPTER 1

MEDICAL CARE FROM AFRICA

In order to appreciate the belief and use of African medical substances and practices, let's explore who the medical caregivers were and what agents and practices were employed.

African Folk Practitioners

African folk practitioners knew customs and traditions of their people, handed down or taught to them by wise and successful caregivers. They relied on intuition and observation of plant/herbal effects, as well as religious or magical folk remedies. Krippner and Colodzin relate four types of folk practitioners whose treatments overlap within the African slave culture. Shamans were spiritual healers that sometimes used herbs to assist in the ceremonies to cure symptoms of illness. Spiritualists used herbs to contact the spirit world as well as other mediums. Esoterics relied on occult approaches to treat illness, which included acupuncture, meditation, and herbs. Intuitives were known as faith healers who laid on hands to treat sickness; herbs assisted in this healing process. (2)

The African slave herb or root doctor (folk practitioner) studied medicinal properties of plants and herbs, which grew in the woods and fields of their new home. Africans' stories and traditions included religious, magical plant properties brought from Africa or the Caribbean to North America. This African knowledge of plant properties and treatments were not known in America until the Africans shared it with the European white culture. Some of these practices were Cesarean section surgical procedure, use of citrus fruit to fight scurvy, practice of midwifery, and inoculation with smallpox scabs. The African slave incorporated this medical knowledge along with the new plants that he experimented with in America. (3)

109

The herb doctors retrieved plants and herbs from Southern gardens, forests, swamps, and fields. The medicine and techniques that they brought with them were adapted to their new surroundings. They investigated, tested, and perfected the use of the new plants found in America to treat both African and white diseases. For instance, the kola nut, a stimulant known in West Africa, was adopted so widely in America that it eventually became the main ingredient in Coca-Cola.

> Not all Americans favorably viewed slaves performing all aspects of their African medical knowledge, especially the spiritual components.
>
> Some whites tried to suppress traditional West African and Caribbean emphasis on spiritual or supernatural forces in the healing process, such as those found in conjure . . . Sometimes the conjurer doctors focused on blood, such as purifying it through herbal laxatives, enemas, colonics, or fasting. (4)

Training

Similar to American colonial medicine, detailed African medicine was taught through apprenticeships to those worthy to learn the secrets. The young and gifted female and male African slaves were chosen to learn herbal and non-herbal techniques. Many were so successful that their fame gained them freedom.

> In 1729, Virginia Lt. Governor Gooch authorized the payment of sixty pounds to manumit an unnamed Negro man. Gooch declared that his mixture of pharmacologically active roots and bark had proved an effective syphilis remedy. (5)

Primus was another slave who won fame for medical achievements, which included a rabies treatment. (6) How valid these treatments actually were in combating syphilis and rabies is highly suspect.

We do know that those white men accepted and placed trust in the African cure administered by those slaves.

Conjurer doctor

Among the African practitioners was the conjurer doctor who used occult practices to control the illness-producing spirits. These male or female Africans held their strength or power within superstition, combined with various "magical" practices and herbal therapy. They used trickery, violence, persuasion, and medical proficiency to increase their reputations among the community. Superstition was a powerful force among the enslaved population. (7)

Hoodoo and Voodoo were two types of conjuring known in the antebellum South. Hoodoo was found mainly in the Georgia and South Carolina coastal country and incorporated magic, herbalism, and divination. This was the typical old-African cultural and spiritual tradition practiced. Voodoo was similar but found in the deep South and had more of a dark occult flair. Even today, Voodoo is practiced in such places as the Caribbean and Louisiana.

Often, the conjuring proved detrimental to the recovery of the sick slave. Not only was he exposed to harmful procedures and dangerous poisonous plants, but there often was a critical delay in seeking prudent and effective medical care. Minges states: "More than any other superstition entertained by the Negroes slaves, the most harmful was the belief on conjurers." (8) There were slave doctors who appeared to be herbalist folk healers who also treated the white race; they were really conjurer doctors.

One such slave was known as Doc. He would give his herbal concoctions to the white family, but for blacks he had his reserved remedies. Doc gave the whites a special tea and the blacks would wear charms made from buttons and Indian rock beads. Much of the power conjurers held over slaves was psychological rather than physical. Superstition was difficult for the white race to understand or condone. (9)

In 1800, the daughter of Thomas Jefferson, Martha Jefferson Randolph, related that her slave, Jupiter, thought he was imprisoned. This man searched for multiple ways to dispel the symptoms and finally sought out a black doctor who gave him a dose of an herbal treatment. While administering the medicine, the doctor offered a suggestion that the drug would either kill or cure him of his imprisonment. This comment was taken to heart when Jupiter began to have a seizure, which lasted eleven hours. He died nine days later. (10) Obviously, the toxicity of the herb was the true culprit but this tale of superstition was recorded and accepted by both races.

Native Americans

The early colonists found that Native American herbs and medicines were critical to the white man's survival. Medical shipments from Europe were rare and arrived inconsistently, thus pharmaceutical drugs of the time were scarce. Turning to the native population, the colonists bought herbs and learned of new cures. Shryock records fifty medicinals adopted by whites from those routinely used by the Native Americans. Some of these worth mentioning were wild geranium used to treat diarrhea; goldenseal to treat thrush, sore mouth, and sore eyes; boneset routinely counteracted fevers; and Jerusalem oak, wormseed, or pinkroot expelled worms. (11)

The African slave doctors acquired knowledge from local Native Americans. Native Americans and African slaves shared their knowledge of herbal remedies. Merging of both cultures' practices emphasized the importance of spirituality in the healing process; they depended on herbs and plants to prevent disease. Native American medicine men doctors gathered roots, herbs, and leaves to make various medicinal teas and compounds. One African describes a Native American healing practice:

> Each year, usually in July, they would have their annual stomp dances. At these stomp dances they would tie shells around their ankles, and beat on a drum made from a cowhide, and dance and sing.

They would usually fast three days, and then would take a medicine that would cause them to vomit, claiming that would cleanse their system and souls of all the impurities, and then they would enjoy the roasted corn and barbecue that was in waiting for them. (12)

Chapter 2
Slave Self-Care

The African American slave had a limited range of choices with regard to healthcare as we have discovered. Many slaves were reluctant to submit to the 18th and 19th century European/white healthcare system and practices. They thought white man's medicine was ineffective against spirit-caused illnesses. Their desire to rely on self-care or African treatments, delivered by African family, friends, or doctors, was seen as a control mechanism by the white medical community and slave owners. Slaves sought out local herbal medicine first as a cure.

Although the slave and white races shared many of the same teas, poultices and caregivers, there was limited knowledge and acceptance of each other's explanations for illness. Written accounts of several herbal treatments were used by both whites and African slaves; these included castor oil, a mild cathartic, and an antibacterial agent. Turpentine, or pine tree oil, was taken internally for colds and rheumatism. Sassafras was considered a blood purifier by slaves but used as a tonic by whites. Some other common items were camphor, digitalis, ergot, and pokeroot. Camphor, taken internally, acted as a narcotic, but applied externally it transformed into a liniment. Digitalis is known even today to regulate the heart's rhythm, rate, and contraction. Ergot caused uterine muscular contraction and expelled the fetus; this was a violent and deliberate form of birth control.

On large plantations with slave hospitals, the master didn't appreciate the slaves abusing the use of these facilities, medicines, or the plantation white doctor. However, these practices were preferred over the slave's self-medication. Most owners permitted a small amount of self-care for minor ailments, but they were quite unhappy when the slave's illness resulted in his or her extreme disability or death. The owner accused the slave of negligence, ignorance, and indifference to their health. As a result, slave doctors secretively provided treatment among the slaves:

> Black home remedies circulated secretly through the slave quarters and were passed down surreptitiously from generation to generation. Most of the cures were derived from local plants; though some medicines contained ingredients that had magical value only . . . The main source of trouble was usually not the misuse of home remedies, but the prescriptions and activities of so called conjure doctors, whose system existed in the South because the enslaved brought it with them from Africa and West Indies. They were viewed as healers of illnesses that white doctors could not touch with their medicines as perpetrators of sicknesses on any person they wished—all through spells. (13)

Some African slaves learned self-care by observing the plantation physician or the owner who read from a medical "recipe" guide. Anyone could learn to perform bloodletting, apply leeches, blister with cupping, or administer caustic drugs.

> Some planters assigned certain trusted slaves to the task of rendering medical assistance to all ailing bondsmen on the farm. In most cases, these blacks simply dispensed white remedies and performed venesection and cupping as learned from the master. This was not complete black self-care, but did represent a transitional stage in which Negroes had the opportunity to apply some of their knowledge of herbs, gained from elders, in addition to white remedies. (14)

Those slaves chosen to be nurses were generally elderly and relied on their own African herbal remedies.

There were interviews conducted during the 1930's with extremely old slaves and their descendants from sugar country Louisiana and Mississippi, who stated slaves cured themselves with roots, medicinal herbs, and additional homemade cures. Many names for the herbs were common and remain known today such as Jimson weed. (15)

Slave medicines proven effective were even added to the white man's professional journals as new *materia medica*. Stories exist where white doctors brought slave doctors to treat and save black patients who were diagnosed as conjure cases. These events were rare since African slave medicine remained secretive, especially within the deep South.

Free blacks relied mostly on self-care because they couldn't afford white doctors and were not eligible for free plantation health care. They couldn't afford the white healthcare system and were not permitted to be treated within the African slave healthcare system.

African Slaves in cotton field, Library of Congress, public domain

Non-herbal or Untraditional Treatments

Folk tales and oral histories are full of usual and suspect medical remedies. Some of those remedies proved effective while others were dangerous and caused more harm.

Prior to the American Civil War, there were many concoctions that modern science scoffed at as absurd. An example was the curing of whooping cough by combining unsalted butter, garlic, lard, and vinegar, which was placed upon the patient's chest. Native Americans introduced the way to stop bleeding with a cobweb and soot poultice that actually worked! Both the African slave and white races adopted this remedy. The slaves thought there were many uses for worms; the most curious was treating earaches by eating stewed earthworms. They also soaked rusty nails in vinegar and drank it to expel internal worms. (16) Worms were obviously of much concern during the 19th century. The African slave called poultices *opodeldoc* and applied them externally for numerous ailments. Radish *opodeldocs* were used to treat headaches, as did those made with nutmeg, and were worn around the neck. Muscle and joint sprains were treated with a clay and vinegar *opodeldocs*. For nail puncture wounds, a piece of fat with a penny placed over the wound would cure blood poisoning. Coal dust mixed in salt and then warmed treated rheumatic joint pain.

Both African and white races living in Texas had similar untraditional non-herbal remedies for common ills during antebellum times. Rheumatism was treated with vinegar poured into a bottle containing red ants and shaken; it was to be drunk or applied externally. Smoking coffee grounds would cure hay fever; it is assumed the smoking was done with a pipe. My favorite: a cockroach brewed with water into a tea was guaranteed to cure lockjaw. Nosebleeds required a woolen thread to be tied around the large toe, and another woolen thread attached to a mashed lead bullet and hung around the neck. This would soon stop the bleeding. A simple and pleasant remedy to cure colds was to drink plenty of whiskey. To cure night cramping, place your shoes upside down under the bed and cramps will disappear. It probably was as good as placing a knife under the bed during childbirth to cut the pain. The most dangerous treatment of a sprained ankle involved bathing the area in turpentine, set a lighted match to the site, and let it burn for two minutes. Be sure to fan out the flames. (17) It is hard to believe people actually tried these "cures" and believed in them, but slaves were desperate for cures.

Many of the non-herbal remedies involved superstition; coins, beads, and rabbit feet were charms used in both voodoo and conjuring. Of course, the most important ingredient for the charms to work was that the slave had faith in the doctor and his cure.

Foods as cures

Every day food articles were used medicinally and did have true healing properties. For instance, honey was popular in treating colds, coughs, skin infections, and removing splinters. During the American Civil War, bandages wrapped with honey had a higher rate of healing because of the antiseptic properties of honey. Today, honey has been used by traditional medicine to treat burns; it also fights bedsore infections when it is mixed with sugar.

Honey has demonstrated some antimicrobial properties with regard to typhoid, dysentery, and other bacterial infections. (18) Southerners also recommended honey, lemon, and whiskey to treat colds for many decades after the war. Sugar's ability to stop bleeding and encourage healing was well known in the South. (I can remember my Northern grandmother giving me hot water with lemon and honey for a sore throat as a young child).

Whiskey was used as an ancient remedy to treat most any ailment from colds to worms. How much and often this remedy was used probably depended upon how much that person enjoyed 'spirits.'

Vinegar's astringent properties combated fevers and nose bleeds. Today, frequent vinegar and water douches prevent certain vaginal infections. Apple cider vinegar is also a diuretic and aids in reducing cholesterol levels. Slaves would heat vinegar mixed in water before placing it on broken bones. It was also recommended by slaves to treat colds, arthritis, fungal skin infections, hair and scalp problems, insect bites, and itching. (19)

Some remedies were downright dangerous such as using a sugar and kerosene mixture to cure a cough. Kerosene inhaled can result in aspiration pneumonia, seizures, and death. Infant colic was treated with scrapings from hogs' feet debris, boiling the substance with any white material, and administering for flu, colds or cough. Animal manure dried and made into a tea to treat scarlet fever was also tried. People were desperate; few children survived in those days when scarlet fever struck families. Turpentine oil taken orally was a cure for worms but in large doses could result in seizures, vomiting, shock, and death. Today, turpentine is used for certain skin ailments, cough, and congestion; it is a highly toxic and dangerous therapy. Lastly, a dangerous and nauseating practice was the process of urinating on leaves and rubbing this mixture on an infant's mouth with thrush, a fungal infection. It is presumed that the acidity of the urine would kill the fungus; documented results are unknown to this author.

African Slave Family, Public Domain

Chapter 3
Comparison and Analysis Study

We can learn from our history and from the remedies our American ancestors used in the past. Case in point, I reviewed over one hundred medical remedies of the 1800s and chose forty-seven to analyze because of what they claimed they cured. I also chose those I thought were weird, yet interesting. The majority of these herbs/plants were used by African slaves, Native Americans, and Folk Practitioners, even in the early 19th century.

Key Information concerning this study:

The Folk practitioner was defined as Southern or Appalachian in origin. He or she represented the African doctors' practice. The Native American included both Northern and Southern tribes. The African slave was a non-medical person.

Study Questions:

1. Could the plants or herbs be proven valid treatments for specific illnesses through modern science research?
2. Was there a relationship between the three practicing groups to use the same herb to treat the same illness?
3. Was the treatment dangerous?
4. Were there superstitious elements involved?
5. Is there a modern use for the herb? If so what?

Analysis of Data:

1. 68% (32 of 47) were valid treatments.
2. 19% (9 of 47) were not valid treatments.

3. 13% (6 of 47) uncertain if they helped the symptoms or provided a cure.
4. 6.4% (3 of 47) were superstitious beliefs.
5. 28% (13 of 47) were dangerous because of toxicity or extreme caution advised by science.
6. Thirteen remedies were used solely by the African slave; three were used by only the Folk Practitioner; one was used by the Native American.

Study Findings:

*   Relationships: there was a high correlation between African slave and the Folk practitioners' use of the medicine, none between the Folk practitioner and the Native American Indian, and none between the Native American Indian and the African slave.
*   Sixty-eight percent (68%) of the target remedies were supported by pharmacological research as valid treatments for the stated illnesses or symptoms during the 1800s; many of these are in use today.
*   A significant percentage, twenty-eight percent (28%), was discovered to be toxic and highly dangerous to humans. Warnings were to avoid overuse and high levels of toxicity, or it was banned in the United States, as clearly detailed in the Physician Drug Reference (PDR for Herbal Medicine) manual.
*   A high correlation between the African slave and the folk practitioner supports the oral histories that slaves learned and supported the folk practitioner treatments and used them accordingly.

Much of our synthetic pharmaceuticals use some herbs as the base element in modern therapies. There are current books detailing the value of healing herbs and self-help remedies. To be clear, the author does not recommend any of the therapies or alternative medicinal plants to replace traditional medicine or to use any of said information as personal treatment options.

Summary

During the 18th and 19th centuries, there were various approaches to medicine. Folk medicine filled the gap needed for the African slave to survive. He relied on his culture's use of plants and herbs from West Africa and the Caribbean islands. Many of today's herbs continue to be used because of their proven history of medical cures by many Americans.

(See Appendix for comparison of herbal treatment)

PART 8

American Civil War Medicine 1861-1865

". . . that this nation, under God, shall
have a new birth of freedom—and that
government of the people, by the people, for the
people, shall not perish from the earth."
Abraham Lincoln November, 1863, Gettysburg. PA

Overview

Racial prejudice abounded in both the North and South military units. During the war, only white doctors treated white soldiers. When the USCT (United States Colored Troop) were created in the fall of 1862, Congress commissioned black doctors to care for them. Nursing was done by mostly male attendants at first and followed the same racial lines, but later black attendants also cared for the white soldiers. This was especially true for the Confederacy when the need for more soldiers was out on the battlefield. Female contrabands and slaves worked alongside the attendants performing various functions. Elite Southerners were familiar with African slaves caring for them. There are many stories of white masters sending their favorite or most trust-worthy black slave(s) to care for the son who went off to war. When the son became injured, the slave remained to personally nurse the young man; if the boy died, the slave brought the body home to the family.

As the Civil War progressed, the white and African slave healthcare system greatly changed. No longer were slave infirmaries and medical college dispensaries able to provide Negro medicine. The majority of Southerners left home to fight in the war. Only the sick houses remained with the mistresses caring for her family and directing the slave nurses to treat the slaves who remained and didn't run off. Both the Northern and Southern white populations suffered terribly from starvation, disease, and other hardships. Local doctors, who had not enlisted or contracted with the government, cared for those families and slaves left behind. Southerners all wondered how they would survive and what would life be like after the war.

Both the Union and the Confederate Medical Departments were ill prepared for how to care for the number, type of wounds, and diseases, which confronted them from the very beginning of the war. Few doctors had surgical experience and even fewer were trained in caring for war-related wounds and diseases. The creation of medical examining boards resulted in replacement of poorly trained "doctors" from the service. The description of butchery and carelessness of doctors came from soldier letters home during the early days of the war.

With limited training and experience in trauma surgery and military medicine, Civil War doctors cared for about three million cases of disease and wounds during the war. There were thirty million Americans at the time of the 1860 census and of that number, four million men would serve in the war. The dead totaled more than six hundred fifty thousand, or 46 percent, of those who fought. Of those dead, four hundred thousand died from disease, or 61.5 percent, while two hundred fifty thousand, or 38.5 percent, died from bullet, saber, or artillery shelling. A twenty-first century historian believes that the mortality numbers were much higher. Soldiers' war-related diseases and wounds proved chronic and deaths at home were not recorded in official war documents.

In early 1861, there were no organized system for rapid removal of bodies from the battlefield, no ambulance service, and no specifically trained persons to evacuate the wounded. Since there were no burial guidelines and after the battle the army moved on quickly, where the soldier died was where he was buried. Identification dog tags had not been invented so there were many soldiers buried as unknowns. Soon, the local cemeteries were filled and no national military cemeteries had been designated as yet. There were no policies or procedures for emergency care, prevention of disease, camp sanitation, or feeding and cooking foods in a nutritious manner. There were a limited number of pharmacological labs to produce medicines in America with most drugs being imported from England; there were even fewer labs located in the South. As the war progressed, the South's supply of drugs became critical with the Union Navy blockade of the ports prevented the importation by England or France.

Carnton Plantation's Confederate Cemetery at Franklin Tennessee, author's photo 2013. Mrs. McGavock cared for Confederate soldiers during and after the Battle of Franklin. After the war, 1300 soldiers who died in that battle were buried in the Carnton cemetery.

In 1861, caring for the diseased and injured was a major problem since there were not enough military or private hospitals; each regiment had their own doctor, military field hospitals had not yet been established.

There were only sixteen military hospitals across the country. By the war's end, the Union had two hundred and four hospitals, while the Confederacy had one hundred fifty. Medical supplies were often insufficient in number or they were never received where they were needed most. Military hospital bedding was used until it rotted and bandages were washed in plain hot water, hung to dry, and reused.

There were only a few Sisters of Mercy located in America who had nursing training in 1861. These sisters' knowledge and assistance was requested by both the Union and the Confederate Medical Departments, once the leaders knew the war would last greater than ninety days. By the end of the war, there were three hundred fifty nursing sisters who provided care to the wounded. As the war progressed, many of these deficiencies were addressed.

Chapter 1
Diseases

The greatest danger to the soldiers did not come from the battlefield but from contagious camp diseases. The camps were notorious for overcrowding and poor sanitary measures. The soldiers endured exposure to extreme cold and heat and poor nutrition in camp. All these conditions increased the risk to contract many contagious diseases.

Some regiments lost fifty percent of their men to disease before ever fighting in a battle. By the end of the war, Federal mortality consisted of 394,557 men dead, with 227,580 dying from camp diseases. Confederate mortality was 289,000 men dead, with 164,000 perishing from camp diseases. Freemon reports that the following were the most common camp diseases experienced during the war: scurvy, dysentery/diarrhea, malaria, measles, typhoid fever, smallpox, venereal diseases, pneumonia, tuberculosis, rheumatism, and tetanus, while gangrene and erysipelas occurred in military hospital settings. (1)

As a result of poor sanitary and lack of proper food preparation, dysentery and typhoid fever were the leading causes of death in camp. Food often consisted of spoiled beef prepared by those who didn't wash their hands. Some who prepared food unknowingly used contaminated water from latrine run-off (latrines were often dug in wrong locations near the camps). Most men prepared their own food using the same equipment, which was improperly washed and stored in filthy knapsacks. Food was exposed to insects, blood, and other germ-infested articles within those knapsacks.

New recruits signed on after a minimal physical exam early in the war. As these new recruits arrived, they experienced smallpox, tuberculosis, and influenza infiltrated camps by the thousands. Exposure to childhood diseases such as chicken pox, measles, mumps, or whooping cough was especially dangerous to men who came from rural America. Their bodies' immune systems never had the opportunity to build up antibodies against these diseases. New soldiers were suddenly exposed to these childhood diseases, which resulted in many deaths soon after arrival in camp. Measles alone killed ten thousand in both the Union and Confederate armies. Early in the war, symptomatic soldiers were not isolated from the healthy men and disease spread quickly throughout the large overcrowded camps.

While recruits from rural areas were dealing with exposure to diseases, the urban soldier's nemesis was exposure to harsh weather by living outdoors in a tent or maybe using only a blanket for protection. The common cold turned into pneumonia or bronchitis and proved deadly with antibiotics undiscovered until the mid 20th century.

Flies, mosquitoes, lice, and fleas carry germs and virus. Their presence was a result of wearing unclean clothing week after week among insect-infested locations. Soldiers were further exposed to stagnant water that contained latrine wastes, fleas, and mosquitoes. After each battle, decomposing dead bodies of humans and horses were plentiful. During Southern campaigns, more than one million men suffered from malaria in the Union army. Although quinine was available, its side effects, such as loosening of teeth, led to soldiers' poor nutrition and other diseases.

The main staples of soldiers' diet were beef and bread, which lacked vitamins, minerals, and roughage. Fresh fruit and vegetables were rare so widespread scurvy occurred in the North and the South; scurvy is caused by lack of Vitamin C in the diet. Many Union soldiers refused to eat the foul-tasting desiccated vegetables supplied by the Quartermaster Department and soon scurvy would have more victims. Scurvy was also prevalent among prisoners of war. Scurvy delayed healing of wounds, which increased the risk of infection and severe night blindness. Army doctors were aware of scurvy's aftermaths and the effects on soldiers' wounds.

Pellagra is a vitamin deficiency disease most commonly caused by a chronic lack of niacin (vitamin B) in the diet. Vitamin B deficiency is present in people who get most of their food from corn or maize. Symptoms of pellagra are sensitivity to sunlight, skin sores, mental confusion, diarrhea, a weakened enlarged heart, and eventually dementia. Pellagra was a common disease found in Southern POW camps where corn products were the sole food given to the captured.

Typhoid fever, also known simply as typhoid, is a common worldwide bacterial disease transmitted by the ingestion of food or water contaminated with the feces of an infected person. Typhoid is caused by the bacterium *Salmonella typhi*. Unsanitary camp conditions and lack of personal hygiene led to contamination of food and water. It can also be found in raw milk. Symptoms come in progressive stages: slow pulse rate, malaise, rosy spots on chest and abdomen, diarrhea or constipation, enlarged liver and spleen, intermittent fever, intestinal hemorrhage, encephalitis, and coma.

It wasn't until after the Civil War that army doctors realized water was one source of typhoid fever. In 1909, Frederick F. Russell, a United States Army physician, developed an American typhoid vaccine. This was the first vaccination program in which an entire army was immunized. Typhoid is no longer a significant cause of morbidity and mortality in our military.

Malaria has been endemic in the South since colonial times. Black soldiers who contracted certain forms of malaria had twice the death rate of the white soldiers. Malaria was not a serious threat to the Union army as long as preventative dosages of quinine were available and the soldiers faithfully took them. (See previous sections concerning the African slave's immunity to malaria.)

Smallpox was no longer as great a threat to the Civil War soldier as the Revolutionary War soldier. The army knew it must do periodic revaccination to prevent the spread of smallpox. The military doctors also knew scurvy patients could not be revaccinated because of the complications that would arise. There were definitely cases of smallpox experienced among soldiers. African slave children born during the war were unprotected from smallpox, since the absent master was no longer available to vaccinate them.

The most deadly camp disease in the war was bloody diarrhea/ dysentery. In 1861, one in one hundred and seventy-eight soldiers died with dysentery. By June 1865, one in twenty-nine soldiers died from dysentery. The mortality rate increased with each year of the war but the actual number of soldiers who became ill with diarrhea/dysentery decreased. This was the result of the weakened general condition of the soldiers on long campaigns, other diseases, exhaustion, and deprivation. "Their efforts to treat dysentery and diarrhea were to no avail." (2)

There were no cures in the 19th century for dysentery/diarrheas. Antibiotics and other drugs to treat disease-specific organisms had not yet been discovered. What modern science knows about infectious diarrheas could fill many pages of this book. I will share briefly some generic but important points:

- Diarrheas are caused by pathogens/organisms.
- There are many diseases that include diarrhea as a symptom.
- Quarantine of patient, bed linens, clothing, and waste products is imperative or disease can spread through the air and direct contact.
- Physiologically acute inflammation exists either in the upper gastro-intestinal or lower gastro-intestinal tract, depending on which pathogen is involved.
- Symptoms include fever, abdominal pain, nausea, vomiting, blood or mucus in stool, extreme frequency of stools, weight loss, and dehydration.
- Therapies include antibiotics, fluid and electrolyte replacement, organism-specific drugs, bed rest, light but nutritional diet, or resting the bowel as physician directed.

CHAPTER 2
DOCTORS

Immediately prior to the war, U.S. Army medical staff had thirty surgeons and eighty-three assistant surgeons. Twenty-one of those doctors resigned to serve the Confederacy while three were dismissed for disloyalty. Doctors who had a military rank or had passed an exam were ranked as **Surgeons.** They performed major procedures such as amputations in hospitals and were generally not assigned battlefield duty but were located at field hospitals. Those with the rank of **Assistant Surgeons** were contracted to the government and served in field stations or first aid stations.

As the war continued, the ratio of doctors treating soldiers didn't improve very much: one surgeon to 133 Union soldiers and one surgeon to 324 Confederate soldiers. By the end of the war, there were 12,000 Union surgeons and 3,200 Confederate surgeons.

> During the struggle and the months immediately following it (the war), more than 12,000 medical officers (regulars, volunteers, and contract) examined over 250,000 wounds and treated more than 7 million cases of disease. In the course of their duties, more than 300 army surgeons died from wounds, disease, or accidents. (3)

Doctors were unaware of what caused diseases prior to the germ theory acceptance. (Dr. Lister of England proposed the germ theory in 1867, two years after the war ended.) Some doctors had faith in certain preventative/sanitary measures but they were not utilized by all of the medical staffs. Sepsis, known as blood poisoning, was common in the war and caused doctors to become alarmed when those cases arose. Doctors didn't understand the complete pathophysiology or how to treat sepsis.

Although disinfectants were known in the medical world, only certain army doctors routinely employed them. Many regular old-school doctors refused to use these agents. Disinfectants are chemical agents used to inhibit the growth of organisms. They are supposed to be used on inanimate objects and not human living tissue.

Throughout the war, boiling or chemical sterilization of instruments was not done. Soiled bandages were rewashed and boiled for the next patient; however, attendants' hands applying the bandages were unclean and contaminated the dressing during application. Washing of doctors' hands between patients might include a quick dip in water, which may be contaminated. Soap was scarce at times among field hospitals and aid stations. (4)

Chapter 3
Wounds

Wound Infections, Antiseptics, and Disinfectants

Nearly all wounds acquired during the Civil War became infected with "laudable" pus. Most wounds became swollen and inflamed with erysipelas. Also known as hospital gangrene, erysipelas was found among Civil War hospitals of the North and South. Erysipelas literally spread from one patient to another, killing along the way; it is a highly contagious and painful disease called St. Anthony's fire. It resembles a severe inflammatory cellulitis caused by a combination of *staphylococcal* and *streptococcal* bacteria. (5)

Persons whose immune systems were sound and their bodies properly nourished could fight bacteria and the wound healed. Once the body's immune system became compromised and unable to fight, organisms entered the blood stream; septicemia and shock would rapidly occur. With circulatory collapse, a rapid and fading pulse and mental confusion preceded death. The Civil War doctor diagnosed this stage as pyemia. (6)

Confederate Surgeon Chisholm correctly identified the conditions that encouraged sepsis:

> Pyemia, a disease very common in Europe and a scourge of their military hospitals, was seldom found within the Confederate states, until it became necessary to mass large numbers of wounded in crowded and badly ventilated wards, as after the many bloody battles of the past three years. (7)

Erysipelas did not travel alone among the wounded. When the wound involved deep tissues, the stage was set for gas gangrene, a different infection that appeared in both armies. Once this organism entered the wound, the tissue rapidly died and turned black.

The causative organisms of gas gangrene were isolated from wounds received during World War I in 1917. The Center for Disease Control identifies the organisms as *staphylococcus aureus* and *clostridia*. *Clostridia* are anaerobic bacteria that thrive in non-oxygenated conditions found in soil and the gut of humans and animals. This bacteria causes botulism, tetanus, gas gangrene, food borne diarrhea, and necrotic enteritis. It is also seen in bacteremia (blood poisoning) meningitis, septic arthritis, brain abscesses, and pneumonias. It is important to note that gas gangrene is NOT contagious for other patients or care givers. (8)

Staphylococcus aureus is a germ that often lives in the nose and on the skin of healthy people but can spread on contaminated hands, skin, and objects. Most infections caused by *Staphylococcus aureus* are skin infections, but it can also result in more serious infections such as blood and joint infections and pneumonia. (9)

Gangrene and blood poisoning were high risk in even minor wounds. Some doctors carried germs from infected wounds to other patients by not washing hands between patients or sterilizing instruments before using them again. Since *Staphylococcus aureus* is found on the skin and in noses, the other soldiers, doctors, and attendants were most likely the carriers of these infections to the wounded soldiers.

Although the germ theory was unknown at this time, educated army doctors were aware of "anumels," or animals as seen under microscopes. They made no observation that these objects were related to the infections. Doctors did believe that a clean air environment would result in less casualties of disease.

Laudable pus was considered a healthy sign for healing by both Revolutionary War and Civil War doctors. Yet when certain antiseptics such as iodine and bromide came into contact with the wound, pus disappeared. This phenomena supported doctors who refused to use antiseptics, since these chemicals prevented laudable pus. Those doctors who did believe in using antiseptics ordered wounds to be bathed in bromide; antiseptics commonly used by the Federal medical department were iodine and bromine. The

Confederate medical department used forms of alcohol and certain plants as antiseptics. (10)

Several doctors wrote about their experiences with antiseptics: Dr. Goldsmith, a superintendent at Louisville, Kentucky, recorded a ninety-four percent cure rate treating hospital-gangrene infested wounds by using a bromine solution during wound-cleansing procedures. (11)

Disinfectants were first used to produce an agreeable odor to conceal foul smells, as they combined with noxious atmospheres. These disinfectants used were burning coffee, sugar, or vinegar. The next class was chlorine, which is a mixture of manganese, salt, and sulphuric acid. Both bromine and chlorine were used to clean unoccupied wards, latrines, and water closets. They also used another very powerful agent, permanganate of potash that rapidly destroyed all putrid organic compounds.

Wound Care and Cleansing

If an artery or internal organ was sutured, a long protruding end of that suture line was left to hang outside the wound. This hanging thread caused many infections or secondary hemorrhage when the line was accidentally dislodged. There had been several accidents where the full dresses pulled out the suture line thread. As a result, women who nursed or visited the ill were not permitted to wear hooped skirts.

> Wounds from the Richmond battlefields took on a sloughing condition at an early period and amidst the destruction of tissue, which followed more or less rapidly, arteries were frequently opened, and fatal cases of secondary hemorrhage were numerous. (12)

Dr. Chisholm, who was one of the few doctors with trauma experience, recommended the use of a nitric acid solution to cleanse wounds and remove sloughing that contained hospital gangrene. The solution was thoroughly applied to every part of the wound; this caused extensive pain but once done a poultice of charcoal, flaxseed, or corn meal was applied. The poultice substance was mixed with turpentine or creosote. The wound was dressed with cotton or lint and then drenched in one of those liquids as well. Once granulation was noticed in the wound, warm water dressings began. (13)

Dr. Chambliss, of Camp Winder Hospital in Richmond, supported Chisholm's cleansing process:

> Nitric acid has been applied in every case of hospital gangrene which has occurred in this hospital during the past year—in every case with benefit, and in most cases with prompt and decided success, which may always be expected as the result, if properly applied. (14)

Later nitric acid was replaced with one of the halogens of iodine, or bromine, that proved to be even more effective. Bromine was not only applied to wounds but also sprayed into the air. Unfortunately, no one thought of sterilizing medical instruments with the bromine.

Amputations

Amputations saved many more lives that would have been lost. It was remarkably effective considering the medical knowledge of that time. With a mortality rate of six percent, over 60,000 amputations were done during in the Civil War. Three out of four operations performed in the Civil War were amputations. An experienced surgeon performed an amputation in ten minutes. The size and caliber of the Minie' ball caused splintering of the extremity bones. It was impossible then as it is now to save the limb once the bone shaft was splintered longitudinally.

If previously amputated wounds became infected with gas gangrene, erysipelas, or necrotizing fasciitis, then secondary amputations would be required to save the soldier's life. Most of those Civil War victims described with symptoms of necrotizing fasciitis did not survive.

Of course, 19th century doctors did not understand the differences between gangrene and necrotizing fasciitis.

Necrotizing fasciitis is known today as the flesh-eating bacteria. It is a fast progressive disease that destroys muscles, fat, and skin tissue. The causative organism is Group A *streptococcus* found in throats and skin of humans. Most people have the mild form seen in strep throat or impetigo. When the organism enters the blood stream and multiplies, it becomes life threatening with a drop in blood pressure and organ failure. Today, thirty-five percent of those cases die when the severe form occurs. (15) The incidence of these Group A *streptococcal* infections can be reduced simply with good hand washing and personal hygiene. The first signs of these infections are swelling, redness, wound discharge, and pain.

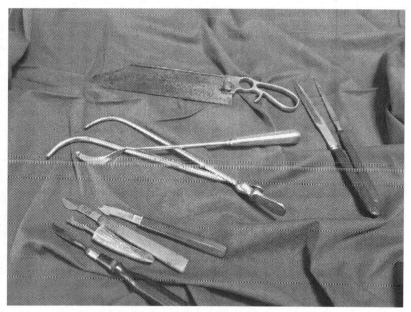

Bone saw, scalpels, knives, and urinary dilators

At the beginning of the war, inexperienced and unscrupulous doctors performed amputations just to gain procedural experience, according to Dr. Chisholm. Some would actually leave the bone sticking through the skin flap. This would result in a high risk of infection and inability to use a prosthesis if the soldier survived. (16)

The most common amputation sites were the hand, thigh, lower leg, and upper arm. Survival depended on the distance of the operation site from the trunk and the amount of treatment delay after injury. The amputation procedure consisted of applying a tourniquet above the site to stop the flow of blood. The surgeon would use a scalpel to slice through the outlying tissue and flesh. Once the bone was exposed, the doctor used a hacksaw-like tool called a capital saw to cut through the bone. Once the bone and flesh were removed, the doctor sutured the major arteries and veins together. A flap of skin was pulled over the wound opening so that eventually an artificial limb could be utilized.

Hemorrhage

Primary or secondary hemorrhage was the "terror" to the surgeon and the patient. Doctors stopped the bleeding initially with digital pressure; if the bleeding persisted, they used styptics and opium. If these approaches failed, then the surgeon resorted to tying or ligating the artery. Dr. Chisholm, a Southern doctor, highly recommended to discard using tourniquets at the hospital level of care. He noted that it wasted time and was ineffective in many cases and it could easily be displaced.

Pvt. Stubblefield a prime example of a poorly performed amputation; note bone sticking from the stump, courtesy of National Medical Museum

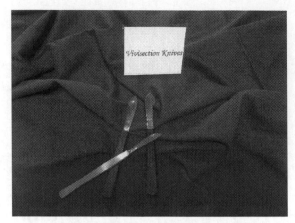

Venesection knives

Sgt. Alfred Stratton of Co G, 147ath NY, Infantry, with
amputated arms, courtesy Library of Congress

**Grave Stone for T. Stonewall Jackson's
amputated arm, Findagrave.com**

The most famous amputation in Civil War lore was that of Thomas "Stonewall" Jackson's left arm. He was wounded by friendly fire at Chancellorsville, VA, in 1863. The arm lies buried near Ellwood Manor, Fredericksburg, and Spotsylvania National Military Park, VA.

Fractures

Long bone fractures were treated primarily with amputation of the limb. As stated previously, the Minie' balls' size caused severe splintering of the bone that even modern medicine cannot salvage. There was a small percentage of those cases which had resections done to preserve some extremity function. Resection, or removal of damaged bone, came with a price; only four percent would survive death from hemorrhage or infection. In the Union Army, there were 174,200 wounded limbs with 30,000 amputations performed. The need for artificial limbs increased dramatically because of the war.

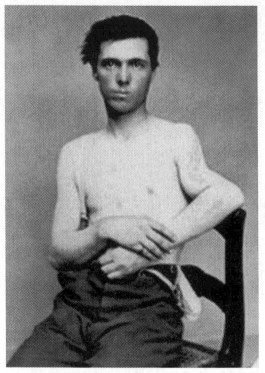

Pvt. Wm. Massy Co I, 7ᵗʰ Illinois wounded Oct. 5, 1864 at Altoona, GA. Left upper arm resection, courtesy of National Medical Museum.

The most experienced doctors performed amputations at the military hospitals. There still exists much controversy concerning the large number of "unnecessary" amputations performed during the war. Yet, Dr. William Williams Keen, well-known 19th century surgeon who served during the war as a medical cadet stated: "Far more lives were lost from refusal to amputate than by amputating."(17)

Civil War army doctors had little experience with traumatic injuries from the new rifles and artillery shelling. Previous wars were fought with smooth bore weapons using smaller round balls with a range of one hundred yards and artillery-fired solid objects. By 1860, rifled muskets fired Minie' balls with .58 calibers with a range of six hundred to one thousand yards. This weapon and ammunition had a tremendous impact on morbidity and mortality rates. The Minie' ball would flatten and cause more extensive wounds shattering bones and ripping ligaments and arteries to shreds. It is no wonder so many men had such crippling injuries.

Attendants and doctors dressed wounds with non-sterilized cotton at battlefield stations. These dresses stayed sometimes for days before the soldier could be transported to a general hospital. Private Richard Ackerman of the 5th New York Regiment was wounded at the Second Battle of Bull Run August 1862. He laid for forty-eight hours on the battlefield and then rode for forty-eight more hours to a treatment area. The delay in treatment resulted in complications, which took his life four months later. (18)

Keep in mind that most of the battles were fought in farm pastures, where animals grazed and their waste products deposited. Organisms that caused tetanus, or lockjaw, and gangrene were living in the soil as spores, ready to attack an open wound.

Jonathan Letterman, Medical Director of the Army of the Potomac from 1862 to 1864, developed a new system where an aid station was located near the battle site. For the first time, contract doctors and/or the stewards performed initial treatments; they prepared the soldier for transport for more extensive treatment at the closest field hospital. This procedure alone saved thousands of Union soldier lives. Letterman's system exists within the US Army Medical Corps today. The Union Army experimented with various wagons, carts, and stretchers to move the wounded rapidly off the battlefield to the field hospital. The Rucker ambulance proved the most versatile of all designs. Supply and livestock trains and ordinary ships evacuated the wounded but were replaced with hospital railcars and hospital ships developed by Northern charitable organizations.

Red Rover Hospital Ship courtesy of NIH.gov

Dr. Henry Bellows, a Unitarian minister, along with other prominent citizens, created the U.S. Sanitary Commission in 1861. The purpose of the commission was to provide an agency that would source basic supplies needed to improve the lives of soldiers that the government felt unable to provide. The commission worked in the North to improve camp and hospital conditions with dietary and medical supplies; this greatly improved Union soldiers' morale and physical health. The South had a more difficult time obtaining supplies because of Union-blocked ports. Southern soldier relief depended on local community efforts, individual volunteers, and family members.

CHAPTER 4
ANESTHESIA AND ANALGESICS

Anesthesia was used in ninety-five percent of the 80,000 surgeries performed; not all soldiers would receive anesthesia. Those soldiers with facial wounds or impaired airways would not receive chloroform during surgical procedures. Anesthesia administration of soldiers with these injuries caused increased risk of breathing cessation and aspiration. Doctors were well aware of the side effects and cautions required with anesthesia.

If there was a delay in getting chloroform, doctors waited to do any major procedure. Chloroform was made with alcohol and sulphuric acid or chlorine powder. Southern labs made their own supply of chloroform when European supply ended. Deaths from chloroform averaged 5.4 per 1000 cases, while deaths from ether were 3 per 1000 cases. So why did the armies not use ether? Being highly flammable, ether was very dangerous when surgeries were performed by candlelight. (19, 20) Ether was used primarily only at the general hospitals.

Some doctors remained a little wary of anesthesia; they knew that it affected the soldiers' appetite and caused nausea and vomiting post-procedure. There were even some who were concerned that anesthesia would delay the healing process and result in more wound infections. This of course was quite untrue. Doctors did learn that whiskey given as a premedication resulted in a smoother induction to chloroform. Whiskey eliminated the pre-excitation phase and thus an easier induction to the unconscious stage.

Doctors also used analgesics for pain relief; alcohol was used to relax the patient preoperatively. Alcoholism was a problem for soldiers during and after the war. Doctors, especially for Northern soldiers, freely prescribed the use of narcotics such as opium and morphine. In fact, there was such an overuse of opiates that many soldiers, from both sides, became addicted. Opium was prescribed for painful diarrhea to stop the frequency of loose stools. Morphine was dusted into wounds or given by hypodermic needle into muscle or veins. There was also occasional use of cannabis for patients with tetanus to stop muscle contractions or headache from head injuries. (21)

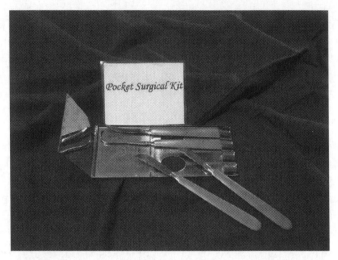

Portable Surgeon's surgical kit, author's photo

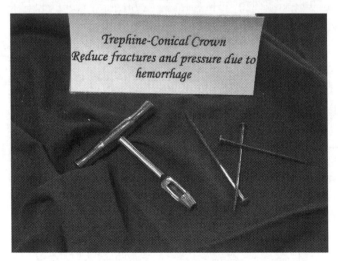

Trephining drill to insert holes in skull to relieve pressure on the brain, author's photo

The following timeline documents the advancement of surgical anesthesia:

- 1831: Chloroform was introduced to alleviate sensations during a surgical procedure.
- 1842: Ether was first used, but not routinely until the Civil War.
- 1846-1848 The first military use of ether was during the Mexican-American war.
- 1853: The hypodermic needle was introduced as a medical instrument.
- 1854: The first local anesthetic was administered with the hypodermic needle. (22)

CHAPTER 5
MEDICAL DIAGNOSTIC TOOLS

Stethoscope

In 1816, R. G. H. Laennec invented the stethoscope, but it's use spread very slowly from Europe to America. Medical students and doctors owned the monaural (one ear) stethoscope by the time of the American Civil War as documented in many case histories. (23) These clinical reports lead us to believe that the same terminology used to describe pathological heart and lung findings remain in use today by doctors and nurses alike. Some of the recorded diagnostic findings were rubbing sound with each heartbeat, crepitus, bilateral rales in lung bases, and increasing heart murmur whooshing.

Further, case studies reveal that Civil War doctors used the stethoscope to diagnose pathological anatomy without sophisticated technology and studies. Such technology used in the 21st century is the electrocardiogram, computed tomography (CT), cardiac calcium scoring, echocardiogram, magnetic resonance imaging (MRI), Holter monitoring, x-rays, ultrasound, and laboratory blood studies. Both medical departments placed the stethoscope on their supply list, available for doctors at field stations and hospitals to use.

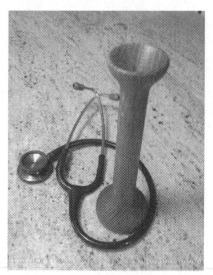

**Monaural stethoscope used in the Civil War compared
with the author's nursing Littman stethoscope**

It was not until the mid-20th century that the stethoscope was invented which required two ears to listen and improved the ability to hear certain sounds. Both nurses and doctors routinely use the stethoscope as standard of care in everyday modern clinical practice.

Thermometer

The thermometer used in the 19th century was invented by Gabriel Fahrenheit in 1720. By 1851, Dr. Phillips of Oxford, England invented a self-registering model that used mercury and a small air bubble. The thermometer was used during the war mostly in the large military hospitals. There were only eight instances of recorded cases that noted a fever was measured and recorded in degrees. (24) Generally, statements such as "patient was hot" were written throughout the official records. It was not until 1868 that Karl Wunderlich demonstrated the importance in compiling temperature charts to aid in diagnosis. Temperature charts eventually became standard practice for doctors and later standard of care for the professional clinical nurses. Temperature charts are graphed data of the patient's temperature over a period of time, used to detect patterns or trends to aid in diagnosis.

Fevers were entities of their own; that is, they were viewed not as symptoms but as diseases. As medicine became more scientific-evidence based, this changed to modern medical theories of disease diagnosis and treatment.

Microscope

With the development of the achromatic microscope, American medical schools incorporated their use and derived knowledge through medical school programs. Alfred Jay Bollet, MD clarifies the role of the microscope during the war in his book, *Civil War Medicine: Challenges and Triumphs.* He states that the Civil War doctors' knowledge of medicine was current with international standards of the day, which includes both the microscope and ophthalmoscope. He documents clear evidence that Civil War doctors used the microscope in both field and general hospitals. They were able to identify pus corpuscles and chains of bacteria, which they erroneously thought were normal in most instances. Both urine and stool samples were examined. (25)

Union Surgeon General William Hammond hired Dr. Joseph Woodward, now a field surgeon, to work in the new Army Medical Museum. Woodward prepared tissue slides with stains, and microscopically examined samples of diarrhea.

Ophthalmoscope

The ophthalmoscope was used by civilian doctors who specialized in a new field of medicine called ophthalmology. Bollet states that atropine was used to dilate pupils during ophthalmic examinations. If ophthalmoscopes were available, they were found in certain medical schools and not in field or general hospitals. (26) Civil War Army doctors did not use the ophthalmoscope in their work. Medical doctors gained much knowledge to treat eye wounds by 1864. As a result with most singular eye injury, the other eye would develop a problem called sympathetic ophthalmia (SO).

CHAPTER 6
CASE STUDIES

Case Study W. E. Crolins

Thirty-year old Private W.E. Crolins of Co A, 72nd PA regiment, was wounded by a Minie' ball at Gettysburg on July 2, 1863. He was sent to the Second Corps Hospital near the battlefield after his injury, where he was diagnosed with a compound comminuted fracture of the right arm. Surgeon M. Rizer of the 72nd PA regiment performed Crolins' amputation twelve hours after the injury. He left six inches of bone attached to the shoulder.

On July 29th, Crolins was admitted to Camp Letterman at Gettysburg. He improved until transferred on September 3rd to Satterlee Hospital in Philadelphia, Pennsylvania, the largest military hospital in the North. The amputated arm flap never entirely closed or healed. The Acting Assistant Surgeon Thomas Morton could put a probe up the center of the bone cavity to the head of the bone, which had necrosed and now was quite soft.

On January 8th, the arm under went a second amputation at the shoulder with the entire bone and head removed. Crolins' medical record included the note: "Considerable hemorrhage took place, and some hemorrhage secondarily, but not to any amount, brought on by an attack of vomiting." After the surgeon used silver sutures, the wound was almost healed by February 10, 1864. Crolins was discharged and pensioned on May 3, 1864. He lived to collect his pension. (27)

Case Study Patrick Graham

Patrick Graham was born on November 15, 1817 to a third-generation Scotch-Irish family of Brady Bend, Pennsylvania. He had several different jobs such as timekeeper during the building of the Pennsylvania Canal and a tailor before moving to Johnstown, Cambria County, Pennsylvania.

When Lincoln called for volunteers to enlist for ninety days, friends and families from Cambria and surrounding counties joined as Company E, 54th PA regiment volunteers. Patrick was forty-three years old, married with children, and joined with the rank of corporal. The 54th PA was recruited in autumn of 1861, and mustered in at Camp Curtin, Harrisburg, Pennsylvania, during February 1862. After a brief stay in Washington City, the 54th PA regiment was sent to guard the B & O Railroad and Canal. Following the Battle of Gettysburg, the 54th and other Union regiments pursued Lee as the Army of Northern Virginia retreated from Pennsylvania to Virginia. During this time, Corporal Graham was promoted to Captain of the 54th Co. E.

When the Shenandoah Campaign commenced in 1864, the 54th PA was assigned to General Franz Siegel at Winchester, VA. On May 15th, Siegel's forces engaged Breckenridge's Confederates including the VMI cadets at the Battle of New Market, VA. It was about 3 pm at New Market, that Captain Graham was struck with a Minie' ball in the left eye. He was knocked unconscious and several of his company leaned him against a tree thinking Graham was dead. Soon, Graham was forgotten during the mad rush of retreating Union troops

Long into the night, residents from New Market combed the battlefield looking for survivors and bury the dead. Captain Graham was found alive by a female Union sympathizer. He was transported by wagon to the nearest Confederate hospital facility located in Harrisonburg, a converted female academy. A highly respected local physician treated Graham and performed an enucleation of the destroyed left eye and sewed the eyelid closed. The Minie' ball was not located by the doctor. Captain Graham would later tell his family how he spit the Minie' ball that had exited his soft palate into his mouth. The conical ball had entered the left eye and eventually worked through the roof of his mouth.

After several days, Graham was transferred to Staunton, VA, where a train took him to Lynchburg, Virginia. Here, Graham was triaged and sent on to Richmond's Hospital #21 for Union prisoner of war officers.

Capt. Patrick Graham, family photo.

After receiving further medical care in Richmond's POW hospital, Captain Graham was sent by rail to the sick and convalescent hospital at Camp Asylum, a Southern prisoner of war camp located at Columbia, South Carolina. Graham remained a prisoner until his parole on March 1, 1865, and was mustered out on March 12, 1865 at Camp Parole, Maryland.

Graham returned home and served as justice of the peace and later as alderman in Johnstown, PA. He sometimes wore an eye patch but was never able to have a prosthetic eye due to the socket damage that had occurred from the wound. Soon after the war, Graham's wife died; he remarried and lived a long happy life. He was buried in 1904 with military honors at the GAR plot of Sandyvale Cemetery in Johnstown. The story doesn't end here. During the flood of 1937, all of Sandyvale Cemetery's graves were washed away.

It was fortunate for Graham to have been an officer when he was captured. Other non-officer soldiers of the 54th PA captured at New Market were sent to Andersonville's Camp Sumter. Patrick Graham was my four times great-grandfather. His daughter, Martha, (by his first wife) married one of the soldiers in Graham's Co. E, my three times great-grandfather who also survived the war.

Because soldiers exposed most of their bodies when firing rifles/ muskets, their eyes were very vulnerable to injury from shrapnel, debris, dirt, and bullets. Assistant Surgeon, General George Otis, studied eye injuries during the war. He found that two-thirds of 1,190 soldiers had loss of one eye due to eye injuries. Of those subjects, five percent lost sight in both eyes or died from their wounds. (28)

Although ophthalmology was a new specialty, Civil War doctors knew that if foreign bodies were lodged in the eyeball, removal of the eye was a necessity to prevent sympathetic ophthalmia. SO is an inflammatory condition, which affects both eyes and occurs after a penetrating injury to one eye. The injured eye is known as the exciting eye while the uninjured eye is the sympathizing eye. SO has a gradual onset that progressively worsens. It occurs in ninety percent of the eye wounds within the first year. The main treatment today is early aggressive intravenous anti-inflammatory medication and immunosuppressive drugs, steroids. The cause of SO some believe is an attack by one's own immune system against eye tissue. (29)

In 1851, Herman Helmholtz, German physician and physicist, invented the ophthalmoscope, but Ophthalmology was not founded until 1862; this specialty was not available in field hospitals. Confederate soldiers with eye injuries received specialized care in a "specialty" ward located at Forsythe, Georgia, by 1864. There was also an eye hospital in Athens, Georgia, founded by Bolling A. Pope. In the North, Wills Hospital of Philadelphia treated diseases of the eye, and Dr. William Norris established an eye and ear department at the University of Pennsylvania, Philadelphia, Pennsylvania.

Case Study William Taylor

Dr. William Henry Taylor was a Confederate Assistant Surgeon for the 8th VA and 17th GA Infantry Regiments. He received his medical degree from the Medical College of VA in 1856. For six months, he was stationed at several Richmond Hospitals and promoted to surgeon status on August 31, 1864. Taylor served during the Battles of Gettysburg, Malvern, and Saylor's Creek.

Taylor related in his memoirs the Confederate view of military medicine given to the troops while in camp and on the march:

> The rigid antiseptic notions of these days (1906) did not enter our heads. We had correct ideas as to ordinary cleanliness and decency, and we policed the camp in accordance with them, but there was no excessive care, nor anything approaching the refinements of present-day sanitary science—such as were applied during and after the Spanish war. Yet the contrast in the results accompanying our crude methods to those attained in the later war is most obvious and most remarkable . . . . Early in the morning we had sick call when those who claimed to be ill or disabled came up to be passed upon. Diagnosis was rapidly made, usually by intuition, and treatment was with such drugs as we chanced to have in the knapsack and were handiest to obtain . . . On the march my own practice was of necessity still further simplified, and was, in fact, reduced to the lowest terms. On one pocket of my trousers I had a ball of blue mass, in another a ball of opium. All complainants were asked the same question, 'How are your bowels?' If they were open, (meaning loose stools) I administered a plug of opium; if they were

shut, (meaning constipation) I gave a plug of blue mass . . . The prevailing diseases were intestinal disorders, though we had a share of almost every malady. Occasionally we suffered seriously from measles. Smallpox was effectively kept in check by vaccination . . . As alcohol liquors were indispensable on a battlefield, it is conceivable that the sudden and complete vanishing to which they were liable might at some time prove to be a very serious matter . . . We were devout believers in the old medical aphorism which declares that wine is the milk of age . . . old age, middle age, any age. (30)

As an assistant surgeon at Gettysburg, he was among the battle line during a fierce cannon onslaught by the Federal artillery. He received a missile wound in the gluteus maximus (buttocks). Surviving the wound, he hobbled away to examine his injury. Finding that he lost only "three or four cubic inches of tissue," he returned to the field station area to continue to treat the wounded. At the time of Lee's surrender at Appomattox, he was surgeon for the 19th VA. After the war, Taylor returned to Richmond to practice medicine. He died on April 14, 1917.

CHAPTER 7

NURSING DURING THE AMERICAN CIVIL WAR

Nursing started by women caring for their sick family members; it is one of the oldest of arts. There is little recorded about American nursing prior to the 1800's, since it was mostly done in the home or in Southern plantations by mistresses or designated slaves.

At the outbreak of the Civil War in 1861, the Union and the Confederacy had no army nurse corps, ambulance service, field hospital service, or organized medical corps. Sisters of Charity, Sisters of Mercy, and Daughters of Charity were the only trained nurses in America. The nursing sisters were unique among the thousands of women and men who cared for the sick and wounded of the war. Many religious orders volunteered and provided nursing care in their own religious hospitals, Army general hospitals, and on the battlefield.

**Sisters of Charity and African Slaves Caring
for Soldiers, Library of Congress**

During the early 1800's, there was a strict taboo against women working outside the home, especially in the South. The war was the motivating factor that drove women out of their homes of tranquil domesticity, and into the world of patriotic self-sacrifice in the form of loving care for defenders of their country. Many women of the North and South were from socially prestigious families who had strong political beliefs and educational backgrounds. Yet, all types of women worked full-time at military hospitals for pay. The women gained personally by supplementing their income for their families and increased sense of self-worth for themselves. The soldiers' morale improved, as did their physical care when administered by women.

As the war lengthened, attitudes began to change about women providing nursing care to strangers. Although women's duties were generally restricted to feeding, overseeing prescribed diets, and writing letters for the patients, they became most valuable to both patients and doctors alike. With time, more evidence surfaces that the female nurses assisted with wound care, dressing changes, and medication distribution.

It was not uncommon for family members to come to their sons', husbands' or fathers' bedsides at the hospitals after battles. Most notable of these was Walt Whitman who, after caring for a family member, stayed to care for Union soldiers in Washington City. Wives of men who followed the armies through the war would "pitch in" and provide nursing care right along with the male attendants. In both armies, recovering wounded soldiers or those with invalid status provided the direct nursing care to their fellow sick or wounded brothers. Proving this to be an inefficient use of fighting men, women, or freed black, women and men were hired to provide basic needs for the wounded and sick at the military and field hospitals. Southern slaves were generally hired out by their masters, who were paid by the government to work for the Confederate Medical Department.

During the Gettysburg campaign, the Federal government wanted women to serve temporarily in field hospitals for a few days or weeks. Some women decided to continue nursing with the army. After the war, many of these women would apply in late 1890's to the Federal Government for a pension.

Hundreds of other women and men appeared in camps offering to give aid and sustenance to the sick and wounded, mainly when the war came to their part of the country. Whether they had nursing experience or not, they came and provided physical and emotional support. Later, records reveal that more than twenty-one thousand Northern women acted as nurses and were involved in some form of care during the war. There are some who believe that more than ten thousand women acted as nurses in the South. It is unknown how many of these women opened their homes to sick, wounded, or recovering soldiers to be used as hospitals and convalescent centers. (31)

Much writing exists telling of Clara Barton, Dorothea Dix, Harriet Tubman, Kate Cummings, and women from both the North and South who provided nursing care to the wounded during the war. (This volume will not delve into their sacrifice at this time but is reserved for a personal future writing devoted to them.)

The North established a sanitary commission, a superintendent of nurses, and the Women's Central Association to initially coordinate all Northern relief and training of women as nurses. The South had neither a sanitary commission, a director of nursing, nor a training program for the want-to-be nurse. Southern doctors recognized how the female nurses affected the healing process of the Southern soldiers. Dr. Chisholm writes:

> In general hospitals, the blessings of a woman's care, her ever-watchful eye and soothing words, her gentleness and patience, have added largely to the comforts of the sick. The experience of Confederate hospitals, in recognizing the vast amount of good which female nurses accomplish, and the incalculable service which they are capable of performing, when judiciously selected and properly organized, is a sufficient reason why they should be attached to

every hospital, and especially in times of war, when there are many and peculiar services cannot be dispensed with. To the surgeon, a good, kind, reliable nurse constitutes more than half the treatment of the sick. It is with the most serious cases that there are advantages in nursing are best displayed. (32)

As earlier stated, nursing was performed by nursing sisters, male attendants, recovering soldiers and contrabands. Some nurses assisted the doctors during surgeries and changed dressings. The hospital steward administered any medication ordered by the surgeon. He also was charged with the administration of the hospital and nursing staff.

The South hired females as matrons for their hospitals; they supervised the cooks and the preparation of the diets for each individual soldier. Many of the matrons would write family members of the death of their loved ones. Volunteers would often write letters for the soldiers to family and provide psychological support as needed. As the war progressed, employed female nurses were trained in dressing of wounds, administering prescribed medications and herbal teas, and applying poultices; a few women wrote about these duties in detail. The armies could not provide enough trained male attendants to do these crucial tasks. The female slaves or contrabands cooked, cleaned floors, washed utensils, and did laundry. They sometimes assisted the male attendants in direct nursing care of Northern soldiers but mostly cared for the colored troopers.

Once the war ended, many women went back home to continue with their lives, while others pursued medical or nursing careers. Women of the North had a taste of self-actualization that drove them to search for professional opportunities. Most women of the South returned to desolation with few having intact homes and families; survival was the goal. Perhaps some went North to also search for other opportunities.

The experiences during the war demonstrated how inadequately prepared the country was to care for the ill and injured. This awareness grew into a public demand for trained nurses. This attitude was supported and encouraged by many of the women who had served in the war.

After the war, Dr. Samuel Gross, chairman of a committee on training of nurses, presented a paper at a meeting of the American Medical Association detailing the neglect of trained nurses found in the United States. The report made recommendations concerning hospital-based nurse training schools and formation of nursing societies. (33)

The first nursing schools in America opened eight years after the war ended. They were modeled after Nightingale's English training school at St. Thomas Hospital in London. In 1873, a famous trio of American nursing schools developed: Bellevue Training School in New York City, Connecticut Training School in New Haven, and Boston Training School in Massachusetts. (34)

Florence Nightingale could have little foreseen the new era dawning for suffering humanity, and the benefits nursing would bestow upon future generations.

PART 9

Revolutionary Advancements

*Medical science has proven time and again that
when the resources are provided, great progress in the
treatment, cure, and prevention of disease can occur.*
Michael J. Fox

Overview

What is a revolution, what does it consist of, and who does it impact? The *New Oxford American Dictionary* defines a revolution as a dramatic and wide-reaching change in the way something is organized or in peoples' ideas about it. To revolutionize is to change something radically or fundamentally.

Certainly, the changes documented in the treatment patterns and ways of thinking about providing care during the Civil War were revolutionary. These changes led to the fundamental American medicine of the next two centuries.

Additionally, dramatic changes to the African slave healthcare system occurred with the end of slavery in the South. No longer would plantation sick houses, medical school dispensaries, or slave infirmaries provide Negro medicine paid for by slave owners or slave traders. Money, food, and other resources were scarce for both the white and the black populations in immediate post-war South.

CHAPTER 1
ORGANIZATION

The most significant and far-reaching Northern medical innovation was Jonathan Letterman's new system. It proved to be a rapid and efficient method to transport the wounded, which saved many lives. Dr. Letterman's primary focus was on three areas: standardization, medical chain of command, and a separate ambulance corps. (1) Medical supplies and how they were delivered to medical corps were standardized so that any surgeon could practice his skills among any regiment. This was accomplished when all ambulance and supply wagons were set up alike.

The new ambulance system was commanded by the medical corps officers rather than the Quartermaster Corps. The ambulances only evacuated the wounded and they would not haul troops and supplies. Medically trained men staffed the ambulances; no longer would cooks and musicians be recovering the wounded from the battlefield. The newly trained crews assisted in the care of the wounded as they were transported to field hospitals. However, not all of the Northern armies employed the entire new system.

Dr. Letterman's system was initiated at the Battle of Antietam, or Sharpsburg, in September1862. (2) Here, the system's weaknesses became apparent. After certain changes and education, system reforms proved invaluable at the Battle of Gettysburg in July 1863, when the Letterman system worked to its full potential. At Gettysburg, the number of ambulances proved most effective. The availability of supplies and improved communication resulted in improved care of the wounded, as seen in less delay and efficient treatment during each day's encounters. The system also helped to prevent onset of infections and loss of blood volume onset, thus fewer soldiers died from shock. (3)

> Shock . . . leads to reversible ischemically induced cellular injury. If the process is sufficiently severe

or protracted (it) ultimately results in irreversible cellular and organ injury and dysfunction. (4)

The new Letterman system included a more efficient method of triage. Triage, sorting casualties into priorities for care, remains a fundamental principle in modern military medicine. It was applied at all levels of medical care. When Letterman's system shortened the time for the hemorrhaging wounded to be treated, it prevented hypovolemia. Hypovolemia remains the most common cause of death among those killed in action during military conflicts. Blood is the gold standard fluid of choice in uncontrolled hemorrhaging shock, something that was not available during the Civil War. There were two recorded cases in the official records of a few ounces of blood infused with one patient surviving. (5)

Elements of Letterman's system provided the foundation of America's military medical system. He could not have imagined that his work would affect so many thousands of lives.

CHAPTER 2

NURSING ADVANCES

"Nursing was at first an occupation, then a vocation,
and is now taking its place as a profession."
Minnie Goodnow Nursing educator,
World War I nurse and pioneer in the
field of textbook writing. (6)

The female nurse was now socially permitted to care for "strangers" outside the home. She had demonstrated her skill and necessity during the war. The value of the nurse continued to grow as women graduated from American nurse training programs. They demonstrated their worth again in the Spanish American War, which led to a permanent Army Nurse Corps. (7)

It is estimated today that there are:

2,824,641 Registered Nurses and 690,038 Licensed Practical Nurses within the nursing workforce during the 2008 to 2010 time period. Based on the size of the U.S. population during this period, this equates to 921 RNs and 225 LPNs per 100,000 members of the population. (8)

Both males and females are educated today as nursing professionals. The American Nurses Association recommends the BSN degree (Bachelors of Science in Nursing) as basic education for the registered nurse.

No one from 1865 could possibly imagine the world of nursing in 2013! The revolutionary advancements in monitoring of vital signs and high technology is used by both nurses and doctors. The knowledge and utilization of data, produced by these technologies, guides the decision making by nursing and medical professionals. Yet, the nurturing and caring component of nursing care is just as important today as it was during the Civil War.

Chapter 3
Surgery, Treatments, and Specialization

Few surgeries were performed prior to the war in America; only a few military doctors had experience with surgery. Confederate Surgeon Dr. Julian Chisholm viewed the care received by the wounded in several European battles prior to the American Civil War. His manual written in 1863 gave specific details to guide the Confederate doctors in surgical techniques, wound care, cleanliness, and various hospital staff duties. (9) Much of what he addressed would reveal the progressive approach doctors provided in the traveling Confederate field hospitals.

In the Union Medical Corps, Dr. Letterman requested a board of experienced doctors to review each soldier who required an operation at hospitals. This ensured that through skilled assessment only necessary surgeries would be ordered and performed by expert doctors. (10) This was the beginning of consultative medicine and medical necessity.

Surgeries improved and new approaches in orthopedic, plastic reconstruction, chest, abdominal, neurological, and eye surgeries were developed. Not only were new techniques created but also equipment was improvised to suit specific operative conditions. Confederate Dr. Hunter McGuire, Stonewall Brigade Medical Director, tells of innovative substitutes he used:

> The pliant bark of a tree made for him a good
> tourniquet; the juice of the green persimmon as a
> styptic, a knitting-needle, with its point sharply bent
> as a tenaculum, and a penknife as a scalpel . . . (11)

Doctors had many opportunities to treat neck wounds and breathing problems soldiers experienced; official records state that tracheostomies were performed in at least twenty cases. (12)

It was not until the Civil War that arterial ligations were known to the medical world. Earlier attempts by doctors during the Crimean War were not successful. The American doctors not only used arterial ligation but also performed it on vessels never accessed previously by any surgeon. The procedure was risky and the conditions under which doctors operated were dreadful. Yet, the Civil War doctor became proficient as they developed their skills through innovative techniques.

Another medical advance was nerve suturing of major nerve injuries within the extremities. The immediate effects of a nerve wound were shock, paralysis, and referred pain. If these continued, they caused serious outcomes for the soldiers. Such cases encouraged research to begin at Turner Lane Hospital in Philadelphia by Dr. S. Weir Mitchell, George R. Morehouse, and William W. Keen. Shock therapy was used on paralytics and electricity was also ordered as a quieting counter-irritant on painful nerves. They also tried leaches placed along the nerve pathways. Atropine and morphine injections were used as well during these experimental treatments.

Neurosurgery grew at an alarming rate because of the number of massive head traumas. Although trephining was known from ancient times, the success and scale was virtually unknown in the 19th century. Northern doctors attempted two hundred trephining procedures with a success rate of forty-three percent. (13) Other neurological care of concussions, depressed skull fractures, non-exiting bullet wounds, and comatose patients were studied and treated with varying degrees of success.

Both the Federal and Confederate Medical Departments recognized when the wounded were in a state of shock, and no surgery should be performed until "sufficient reaction has taken place to enable the patient to bear the additional shock and loss of blood." (14) This in itself was a drastic change that saved more lives than we will ever know. Stabilization of the patient's vital signs is a hallmark in emergency care today.

Amputations, in the beginning of the war, had an objective to avoid septicemia. Doctors amputated limbs immediately when soldiers were brought from the battlefield, even if shock was present. Union Medical Director Frank Hastings Hamilton, a renowned surgical professor, proposed that the first six hours represented a state of shock, and the rest of the twenty-four hours amputation was advised. This was a new thought and method of practice. (15)

When comparing mortality rates from amputations between the Union's 26.3 percent and Franco-Prussian War's 76 percent five years later, data supported that early amputation within the first 24 hours after the shock stage was key to success. (16) The expanding market of artificial limbs developed as a result of the vast number of amputees.

> Two years after the war, the Federal Medical Department authorized the purchase of 4,095 prosthetic legs, 2,391 arms, 61 hands and feet. For many former Confederate states, prostheses constituted the largest single expenditure in their postwar budget since the Federal government provided no pensions or medical care for veterans. (17)

The advancement of rehabilitation medicine was spurred by the overwhelming demand for prosthetic devices. Rehabilitation consisted of finding a suitable prostheses, assisting the patient with his acceptance and successful use of the artificial limb, and adjusting to a new lifestyle. Those who could actually be fitted properly to use a prosthesis were fortunate. Many amputated stumps had either protruding bones or ragged scar tissue that resulted in extreme pain with a prosthesis and could not be adapted to use any type of prosthetic. The Confederate war veteran with amputations showed them as a "badge of honor" for the cause. (18)

Maggot therapy, used by both medical departments, was a new innovation that was soon forgotten after the war. Dr. Joseph Jones noted that maggots destroyed diseased tissue and left the wound healthier and healed faster. This was especially noted in gangrenous wounds. Maggot therapy has come back in fashion for certain wounds and open bedsores during late 20th and early 21st centuries.

Soldiers with chest wounds had a bleak prospect for survival. A clinical trial to test closure of sucking chest wounds was undertaken by Union Assistant Surgeon Benjamin Howard. As air is being sucked into the wound, the lung collapses and oxygenation is fatally compromised. Howard's method used layers of bandages coated with a chemical to prevent air from entering the wound. (19) It had some level of success in treating soldiers with this type of wound.

Dr. Chisholm records the use of a trocar and cannula to evacuate pus or fluid accumulated in the chest's pleural cavity of wounded soldiers. (20) The purpose was to lessen the atmospheric pressure and fluid compressing the lung. Today, this concept has expanded to use underwater seal drainage and negative pressure with suctioning. This procedure is commonly found in critical care units of military and general hospitals.

Generally, abdominal wounds were considered fatal, but during the war doctors learned to repair torn intestines and sew the ends together again. According to Bollet, they learned to do this by reading both American and European textbooks, in addition to developing their own techniques. The use of chloroform as an anesthetic allowed for deeper surgical exploration.

Although plastic or reconstructive surgery was a new concept, there were twenty-two civilian doctors who performed reconstructive surgery during the war. The Federals recorded thirty-two plastic operations done by using facial flaps. The Confederacy perfected wiring of the jaw to treat mandibular fractures. Both of these procedures were innovative and provided models to guide the development of the procedures used today.

The armies had dental doctors who performed the usual filling and extracting of teeth; they also worked with fractured bones of the mouth. The Union Army did not recognize dentistry as a separate field; but the Confederacy did recognize the value of dentistry as a separate entity. Cunningham records that Dr. James Baxter Bean, an Atlanta dentist, performed amazing dentistry on maxillary wombs using an interdental splint. Confederate Surgeon General Moore arranged for Beans' splint to be adopted by the Confederate Medical Directors and used in the various Richmond war hospitals.

There were only a few ophthalmoscopes available to the military doctors. Private doctors who knew about this new specialty had access to this tool. Doctors were familiar with how to prevent sympathetic ophthalmia, use atropine to dilate the pupils, and treat glaucoma with iredectomy. Because of the large number of facial trauma with eye injuries, the ophthalmology specialty grew during the war. It continues today. Artificial eyes became a unique medical business during and after the war providing cosmetic enhancements for the young male soldiers.

CHAPTER 4
ANESTHESIA

Prior to the administration of chloroform anesthesia, Dr. Chisolm recognized that morphine given by hypodermic syringe or oral opium would enhance the effect of the chloroform. With either drug, soldiers experienced less fighting and thrashing during anesthesia induction and awoke much easier. He also supported the routine use of anesthesia during "serious painful operations." (21) The use of chloroform, from the beginning of the war and throughout, proved valuable in the surgical realm. Anesthesia was found to help during wound irrigations and treatment of persistent muscle spasms that occurred with tetanus.

Military doctors in the field today are using rapid sequence induction as standard of care. They use fast acting hypnotics and neuromuscular blocking agents to facilitate rapid airway control. Sedation, amnesic, and analgesic levels are maintained with intravenous administration of these drugs. The Civil War was certainly a testing ground for anesthesia and led the way to painless and safe surgical intervention. (22)

Chapter 5
Hospitals

The large military hospital concept was created by Union Surgeon General Hammond in 1862, it was a wonder of the medical world.

> During the four years of the war, the General Hospital cared for 1,057,523 white soldiers, with a mortality rate of only 8%, which was the lowest ever recorded for military hospitals. The rate was even lower than many civilian institutions at the time. (23)

Overcrowding from the battles of South Mountain and Antietam resulted in the need for large pavilion-style general hospitals; they used the open-air concept as described by Florence Nightingale in her publications. The large general hospital concept was used by both the North and occupied South. By 1863, hospitals became light, bright, and well ventilated.

The new Northern field hospital concept consisted of tents and not buildings. The wounded received care in field hospitals, were triaged, and sent to the large general hospital in large northern cities such as Philadelphia, Washington, Alexandria, Georgetown, and Point Lookout Maryland. The Western Union Army had hospitals built in Memphis, Nashville, Chattanooga, and the Louisville area Jeffersonville, Indiana, was the show place of all Western hospitals. (24)

In the South, principal hospitals were established in most of the states with Richmond as the main hospital center. Naval hospitals were located in Richmond, Charleston, Wilmington, Savannah, and Mobile. The Confederacy's Army of Tennessee became the most innovative operation with the moving of hospitals with each campaign. Southern Medical Director Stout proved to be the organizational wizard of all time.

The South developed wayside hospitals that were established at specific points along turnpikes and railroad junctions. These were used for soldiers going home to recover or had been discharged due to mental issues.

Specialty hospitals for eye and ear injuries, nerve disorders, orthopedic, hospital boats, hospital trains, and convalescent centers were totally innovative facilities needed for the type and number of wounded in the Civil War. Military nurses and doctors today practice at medical centers located all around the world in established military hospitals and floating naval hospitals.

Chapter 6
Antiseptics

Much controversy existed concerning the use of antiseptics by certain doctors in the war. Dressings and operating instruments were not sterilized by using our methods of gas or steam. Still, the attempt was made by both sides to incorporate some form of disinfectants in their practice.

> There was some use of disinfectant by the Confederate medical officers although these were employed altogether on an empirical basis. Nevertheless, turpentine, chlorides, permanganate of potash and diluted pyroligneous acid, and powdered charcoal were applied liberally to wounds by some doctors for the purpose of speeding the process of repair. (25)

As doctors gained experience with hospital gangrene and erysipelas, improvisation resulted in innovation. For instance, Adams records that at Memphis, a particular surgeon insisted that each gangrene patient must have his own sponge, cup, and utensils. If he had more than one wound, then the gangrenous wound would have it's own sponge for cleansing. This was truly a breakthrough in sanitary practices, one that we take for granted in our disposable culture. (26) Some of the disinfectants used during the war are components of hospital and home cleaning/disinfectant agents we use daily.

The key to prevention of spread of germs is thorough washing of hands with soap and water. The Center for Disease Control recommends:

> Keeping hands clean through improved hand hygiene is one of the most important steps we can take to avoid getting sick and spreading germs to others . . . If clean, running water is not accessible, as

is common in many parts of the world, use soap and available water. If soap and water are unavailable, use an alcohol-based hand sanitizer that contains at least 60% alcohol to clean hands. (27)

Many Civil War doctors' memoirs describe the inability to wash their hands properly using soap between cases, while performing surgery. Speed was the most important element when facing hundreds of bleeding wounded.

CHAPTER 7
PROFESSIONAL DEVELOPMENT

Sharing of information among the doctors was encouraged and extremely necessary during the war. Manuals describing surgeries and diseases were published and distributed to military and volunteer doctors to improve the care rendered to the wounded and sick. Dr. Julius H. Chisholm, Dr. Samuel Gross, Dr. Joseph Jones, and Dr. Joseph Woodward were a few of the authors.

> They studied European and American military surgery texts and organized medical societies to learn from each other's experiences and to debate the best methods of dealing with their unprecedented problems. (28)

Northern Surgeon General Hammond proposed:

> Establishing a great graduate school of medicine in Washington for the medical officers of the Army who could be kept in touch with advances in the science. It was to include an army medical museum, whose pathological and surgical exhibits would be contributed by doctors in the army hospitals; and an army medical school operated in connection with the general hospital. After the war the central hospital was to serve as a permanent center of clinical instruction. (29)

Hammond's dream became Walter Reed Army Medical Center and the National Museum of Health and Medicine. The Museum's first curator was Dr. John Brinton who solicited contributions from doctors throughout the Union Army during and after the war. The Museum staff took pictures of wounded soldiers showing effects of gunshot wounds, amputations, and other surgical procedures. All of this valuable information was compiled into *The Medical and Surgical*

History of the War of the Rebellion; the six volumes were published between 1870 and 1883. The museum later conducted medical research. (30)

Walter Reed was built on land designated by George Washington as a military reservation; the hospital has gone through many changes but on August 27, 2011, the hospital closed and consolidated with Bethesda Naval Medical Center. It is now the Walter Reed National Medical and Military Center. (31)

CHAPTER 8

AFRICAN AMERICAN (NEGRO) MEDICAL CARE

There was a high casualty rate among the colored Union troops, thirty-five percent greater than among the white troops. Part of this was due to the neglect by the Federal War Department's commission of only eight Negro doctors and an insufficient number of white doctors to care for the colored troopers. Seven of the eight Negro doctors were stationed in Washington D.C. to care for returning colored soldiers and all of the contrabands who fled the South. These fleeing ex-slaves gathered into crowded camps where medical care was sparse but disease was plentiful. (32) This was an example of the racial attitude held by the North toward the Negro race. Not only were the medical services separate, they were not equal. This was a glimpse into the future healthcare system that will replace the African slave's healthcare system after the war.

Between the time when President Lincoln signed the Emancipation Proclamation and the surrender at Appomattox, one million slaves were freed. Then, in 1865, because of the passing of the 13th amendment, slavery was ended in all states and three million more slaves were freed.

> With the countryside desolated—farms abandoned, bridges destroyed, river levees broken, railroads ruined—tens of thousands of emancipated slaves wandered about uprooted . . . Free as the wind, they drifted into contraband camps and cities where unsanitary conditions and object poverty made them prey to a wide variety of illnesses. (33)

With emancipation and the surrender of the Southern armies, the newly freed Negro living on Southern plantations would no longer receive doctor visits paid by the landowners. If self-help slave medicine didn't work, there was no one to care for the ill. Something had to be done.

In March 1865, the Freedman's Bureau was created to help all Negroes adjust to their new living conditions. The bureau recognized the problem of Negro health; General O.O. Howard, head of the bureau, made Negro medical assistance a top priority. The Freedman's Bureau existed for four and one-half years providing medical relief to one million Negroes by establishing one hundred hospitals and dispensaries. The bureau also provided for teachers and buildings to educate the Southern Negro.

General Otis Oliver Howard

Soon after the war, epidemics of smallpox, cholera, and yellow fever ravaged the South and especially afflicted the Negroes. Smallpox hit the youngsters worse because the young had not been vaccinated and were unprotected. In 1872, smallpox spread through the Negro population of Washington and Alexandria. Memphis was affected in 1873 by yellow fever, cholera, and smallpox. Of course, tuberculosis remained the greatest killer of all populations. Charleston, South Carolina's census of 1866 to 1871 reveals twice as many Negroes died from disease as whites. The Negro children under five years of age died three times that as white children of the same age group. Morais concluded "The health gap that existed during slavery between the Negro and white population in the South tended to widen during the post-Civil War era." (34)

Not everyone was racist. Once the war ended, there were many white doctors who wanted to improve the professional status of the Negro doctors. Many of those Negro doctors sought to advance their careers and go into private practice. Even during Reconstruction, the white doctors helped their Negro colleagues by establishing medical schools; they also were supportive of the Negro doctor to join hospital staffs and become members of the white medical societies. Some Negro doctors were refused admission to medical staffs in the North and South.

During the Reconstruction era, two medical schools opened to train Negro doctors, Howard and Meharry. Howard University of Washington DC opened November 9, 1868 to both white and Negro students. In 1872, it included female students with Dora Speckman the first female to graduate. Meharry Medical College located in Nashville, TN, was created solely to educate Negroes as doctors. Receiving a charter in 1866, the Freedmen Aid Society provided monetary support and the medical department was organized in 1875. Its purpose was to provide college-trained Negro doctors to meet the huge demand for medical care of African Americans. (35)

From 1890 to 1914, there was great concern by Negro doctors about training for Negro nurses; they were well aware of the impact a trained nurse had on the patient's recovery. The New England Hospital for Women and Children in Boston was the first American facility to have a regular course for training nurses. Mary Eliza Mahoney was the first colored graduated nurse in 1879. Even after training, in late 19th century America, it was difficult for all Negro nurses to find employment, but those who did were assigned Negro patients. (36)

PART 10

Epilogue . . .
Post Civil War South

Out of suffering have emerged the strongest souls; the
most massive characters are seared with scars.
Khalil Gibran

Revolutions have a chaotic and unpredictable nature and are
sometimes followed by counterrevolutions, as the situation in the
South. Freed slaves felt that the land they had worked on their entire
lives belonged to them. Many of the old landowning masters still
possessed and controlled the land. Without a labor force, the masters
and the freed people came to an arrangement of sharecropping.
Sharecropping farmers agreed to work another's land and receive a full
share of the final crop after one year.

This gave the freed people more autonomy than slavery. They retained
the right to leave one particular landowner and search for any other
available opportunity. "Emancipation had destroyed the master class,
but it had not significantly altered landownership patterns." (1) The
majority of the freed people continued to work for landowners; many
Negroes had no choice.

Immediately at the close of the war, ex-slave families who were
separated by sale tried to reunite. Throughout the South, Negroes
tried to create a better life within their communities. They strived
to obtain education and healthcare through various governmental
agencies. Reconstruction proved a time of turmoil and controversy

and ended in 1880 with the final withdrawal of Federal forces from the South.

> The Federal government had abandoned the African Americans. Although the 14th and 15th amendments had given them civil rights and voting rights in theory; in fact, many would be prevented from exercising these rights for the next century. (2)

Slowly, the losses suffered in the South from the Civil War were restored, mainly to the white population. Compared with other wars, the restoration was rapid. The South knew that with "cheap labor and freedom from government control, it was possible for individuals to reap large profit in the old agriculture and in new industry." (3)

By 1870, much of the South had recovered and would raise cotton, sugar, corn, and tobacco along with wool and rice. DuBois credits the rapid recovery to the free black laborer of the South. (4) The Negro proved he was industrious and worked steadily and effectively since 1865. These men and women proved to society they were civilized, hard working individuals, who made a difference when treated fairly, respectfully, and regarded as fellow human beings. Their recognition of self-worth as a citizen of America was truly the best revolution that came from the war.

Side note: During the 1950s and 1960s, research concerning the medical differences between the Negro and white population were expanded through clinical studies and governmental funding of various screening programs. The gap between the level of health of African Americans and that of the Caucasian Americans continues to exist today for various socio-economic reasons.

The Civil Rights era of the 1960s changed the African American's life forever, offering more opportunities in medical education and personal advancement, but that is another story. America's present healthcare system is in turmoil with governmental control and regulations. As of this writing, the implementation of the Affordable Care Act (Obamacare) begins in 2014 with unknown consequences for the middle class, businesses, elderly, and ethnic groups.

APPENDIX

COMPARISON OF HERBAL TREATMENT
NATURAL HERBAL TREATMENTS OF THE 1800'S
(References:1,2,3,4,5,6,7,8,9,10,11)

Key:

AS (African American Slave)

FP (Folk Practitioner . . . Black or white)

NA (Native American Indian)

1. **Onion** Quercetin

- **AS:** Treat TB
- **FP:** Upper respiratory infections, gas, worms, diuretic, prevent scurvy
- **NA:** Wounds, pain, malarial fevers
- **Modern Use:** Antimicrobial, antibacterial, very potent Cox-2 inhibitor and anti-inflammatory
- **Cautions:** none
- **Validity of Treatment:** Not for TB but did help in the healing process and ward off scurvy

2. **Garlic** (Active ingredient is selenium, organo-sulphur compounds) allin, allicin, DADS, DATS, ajoene

- **FP:** Earache, fungus infection, urinary tract infection, pinworms, bacterial and virus infections, sore throat, quinsy
- **AS:** Worn around neck to ward off illness, adults drank tea to clear bowels

- **Modern Use:** Reduces serum cholesterol, decrease blood pressure, antiseptic, anti-microbial, anti-viral, anti-flu, cancer chemo-preventive, anti-plaque activity in CVS, PAOD preventive, and treatment agent
- **Cautions:** Overdose can result in selenium poison in
- **Validity of Treatment:** Only as an antiseptic but generally no

3. Horehound

- **FP/AS:** Sore throat diarrhea, whooping cough, asthma, inflammation of the respiratory tract
- **Modern Use:** Expectorant in cough drops, cough suppressant
- **Cautions:** Not to use in pregnancy
- **Validity of Treatment:** Yes for cough suppressant

4. Jimson Weed

- **FP:** Worms, cough, pertussis
- **AS:** Internally to expel worms
- **Modern Use:** Considered a dangerous poisonous plant
- **Cautions:** Not taken internally
- **Validity of Treatment:** No

5. Slippery Elm Red or sweet elm (Active ingredient Mucilage)

- **AS:** Fever, rheumatism, indigestion, sore throat, constipation
- **Modern Use:** Antitussive lozenges, wound healing poultices, inflamed digestive linings
- **Cautions:** Pregnancy, contact dermatitis
- **Validity of Treatment:** Yes for GI and throat conditions

6. Chinaberry Tea

- **AS:** Prevent worms, stomachache, scrofula (TB), boils
- **Modern Use:** unknown
- **Cautions:** Unknown
- **Validity of Treatment:** No

7. Jerusalem oak

- **AS:** Worm expel Tea for chills and fevers
- **Modern Use:** anthelmintic
- **Cautions:** Oxalate poisoning, gastroenteritis
- **Validity of Treatment:** Yes for worms only

8. Dogwood (Active ingredients contain steroids and tannins)

- **AS:** Fevers, substitute for cinchona to treat malaria
- **FP:** Chronic attacks of fever, poor digestion, stimulate appetite, chronic diarrhea
- **Modern Use:** Headaches, fatigue, digestive problems (antispasmodic)
- **Cautions:** Cardiac effect
- **Validity of Treatment:** Not cure for malaria, GI yes

9. Tansy leaf

- **AS:** Poultices for colds, kill worms, encourage menstrual bleeding
- **Modern Use:** Insect repellant, antimicrobial, anthelmintic
- **Cautions:** Pregnancy, not for internal use, liver and kidney damage
- **Validity of Treatment:** Yes to expel worms and abortion

10. Peachtree leaf

- **AS:** Poultices for colds, kill worms, encourage menstrual bleeding
- **Modern Use:** Sedative, diuretic, expectorant used for bronchitis and whooping cough
- **Cautions:** Unknown
- **Validity of Treatment:** No but diuresis may have helped menstrual cramps

11. Catnip

- **NA:** Baby teething
- **AS**: Colic
- **FP:** Colic, colds, fever, migraines
- **Modern Use:** Antipyretic, toothache, anemia, antispasmodic, sedative, diaphoretic
- **Cautions:** Pregnancy
- **Validity of Treatment:** Not for GI or lung illness but has sedative effect on infants

12. Snakeroot

- **AS:** Snake bites, infections, liver and kidney problems, colds, coughs
- **Modern Use:** Expectorant, coughs
- **Cautions:** Pregnancy but not for prolonged use
- **Validity of Treatment:** No just to control cough

13. Sage (Acetylchoinesterase inhibitory activity)

- **AS:** General illness
- **FP:** Loss of appetite, diarrhea, bleeding gums, flatulence, reduces swelling
- **Modern Use:** Antiseptic, antibacterial, astringent, tranquilizing, ant-inflammatory, anti-Alzheimer's memory enhancer, treat yeast infections, loss of appetite and excessive perspiration
- **Cautions:** None known
- **Validity of Treatment:** Yes

14. Raspberry leaf (Active ingredient is tannins)

- **FP:** Diarrhea, pregnancy's morning sickness, female tonic
- **Modern Use:** Astringent, uterine relaxant, hypoglycemia in diabetics

- **Cautions:** Limit quantity in pregnancy, it may cause blood pressure changes
- **Validity of Treatment:** No

15. **Pine needle tea** (Chewing turns into turpentine)

- **AS:** (poultices or Opodeldocs) Colic, backache, carbuncles
- **Modern Use:** Mild antiseptic, oil rubbed into arthritic and rheumatic joints
- **Cautions:** Do not take internally. Can cause brain, kidney and liver damage
- **Validity of Treatment:** Yes only as a topical antiseptic and external rub

16. **Comfrey** (Active ingredient Allantoin promotes growth of new cells)

- **AS:** Burns, digestive aid, wound treatment (used as a plaster for fractured bones)
- **FP:** bruises, sprains, rheumatism, pleurisy, ulcerative colitis
- **Modern Use:** Salves for healing
- **Cautions:** Large amounts of tea can damage liver
- **Validity of Treatment:** Yes for external wound healing, but no benefit for lungs

17. **Wild Cherry bark**

- **FP:** Cough syrup, tea to treat labor pains
- **AS:** blood tonic, bad colds
- **Modern Use:** Sedative for coughs, bronchitis, and whooping cough, astringent
- **Cautions:** none
- **Validity of Treatment:** Yes for cough, may have calmed mother during labor

18. **Poke root or weed** (Stimulates immune system)

- **FP/ NA/AS:** Skin disease, sores, ulcers, tumors, gout, typhoid fever, rheumatism, cure for smallpox
- **Modern Use:** High Blood pressure, emetic, fever, rheumatism
- **Cautions:** Highly toxic, causes violent vomiting and drop in blood pressure, even death
- **Validity of Treatment:** Somewhat useful but never a cure for small pox

19. **Grape seed** (Active ingredient proanthocyanidin inhibits oxygen radicals) resveratrol, stilbenes

- **FP/AS:** Diarrhea, heavy menstrual bleeding, swollen feet, headache, dysuria, scabies, hemorrhoids, vomiting, Gonorrhea
- **NA:** Headache, dysuria, scabies, hemorrhoids, vomiting, Gonorrhea
- **Modern Use:** Cardiac protective, collagen stabilization, anti-inflammation of blood vessels, reduces ocular stress, PMS, diabetes and retinopathy, Sirt1 modulator
- **Cautions:** None
- **Validity of Treatment:** Yes but not for Gonorrhea

20. **Dandelion**

- **NA:** Chronic ulcers, tuberculosis, flatulence, colic kidney stones, gout, jaundice, biliary stones
- **Modern Use:** Urine infections, liver and gallbladder diseases, loss of appetite
- **Cautions:** Closed biliary ducts, GB infections, ileus, increases bleeding if on anticoagulants and increased risk of high serum potassium
- **Validity of Treatment:** For some kidney and liver illnesses

21. **Hops**

- **NA:** Toothache, sedative
- **AS:** Rheumatism

- **Modern Use:** Sedative for agitated or nervousness, insomnia
- **Cautions:** Linked to hepatitis, contraindicated in depression
- **Validity of Treatment:** Sedative effect only

22. Goldenrod (Berberine)

- **FP:** Colds, influenza, fungus and yeast infections, sore throat, nasal congestion
- **AS:** Fevers
- **Modern Use:** Diuretic, antispasmodic, anti-microbial
- **Cautions:** unknown
- **Validity of Treatment:** Yes for mild cold symptoms

23. Red Oak

- **AS:** Treat diabetes, diarrhea, fever, colds, indigestion
- **Modern Use:** Apply a protective coating on blisters
- **Cautions:** Unknown
- **Validity of Treatment:** No

24. Clove (active ingredient is Eugenol high in cinnamon, nutmeg and basil) isoeugenol

- **FP/AS:** Toothache, nausea, vomiting
- **NA:** Colic, toothache, eye diseases, anorexia
- **Modern Use:** Anti-inflammatory, analgesic, antiseptic, antiviral, antithrombotic, used in dentistry
- **Cautions:** Do not inhale clove oil and not recommended for sedated children
- **Validity of Treatment:** Yes

25. Wintergreen tea/ oil (Active ingredient methyl salicylate)

- **FP:** Antiseptic, asthma, arthritis, pleurisy, neuralgia
- **AS:** Rheumatoid arthritis, headaches, back pain
- **Modern Use:** Liniments bath additives use synthetically produced methyl salicylate

- **Cautions:** Contact allergies, fatal poisoning with oil internal use
- **Validity of Treatment:** Yes for symptomatic relief

26. **Sassafras** (Active ingredient is cinnamon wood) Safrole free extracts used as flavorings

- **AS:** Venereal diseases, pain, fever, high blood pressure, rheumatism scrofula TB, gall stones, blood cleansing, clear sinus
- **Modern Use:** Antiseptic, topical, insect bites, lice
- **Cautions:** Contains a carcinogen Safrole
- **Validity of Treatment:** No

27. **Lobelia**

- **FP:** Muscle relaxer, induce vomiting, midwives used to help induce labor, used to cure addiction to smoking
- **Modern Use:** Strong antispasmodic, emetic
- **Cautions:** Highly toxic and banned in USA
- **Validity of Treatment:** Some data supports yes during 19th century

28. **Mullin** (Active ingredient is Mucilage) Triterpene saponins (verbascosaponion) flavonoids, acids, glycosides

- **NA:** Cough
- **AS:** Kidney disease, preventative tonic for colds, congestion, infants washed in its solution
- **Modern Use:** Sore throat, may inhibit TB, expectorant, colds, influenza, asthma, UTI's nervous tension, anti-inflammatory, weak diuretic effect (flavonoids), chemotherapy of many cancers
- **Cautions:** None
- **Validity of Treatment:** Yes for respiratory symptoms but not TB

29. **Mayapple** (Podophyllin resin, several glycosides) Podophyllotoxin derived anti-cancer drugs (etoposide and teniposide)

- **FP:** Worms, chronic constipation, mental illness
- **NA:** A cathartic poison
- **AS:** Induce abortion of fetus
- **Modern Use:** Treats arthritis, constipation, narcotic, purgative, chemotherapy of many cancers types
- **Cautions:** Very toxic and not generally used
- **Validity of Treatment:** Yes

30. **Chamomile** Contains many flavonoids (a-bisabolol), chamazulene

- **FP:** Abdominal pain, skin diseases, sedative for anxiety, diarrhea, sleep disorders, infections
- **Modern Use:** Antispasmodic, anti-inflammatory, antihistamine, sedative, eyewash to treat conjunctivitis, antioxidant, wounds, burns
- **Cautions:** Not for pregnant women or anyone with a known allergy
- **Validity of Treatment:** Yes

31. **Balmony**

- **AS/FP:** Worms, gall bladder stones, colic, nausea
- **Modern Use:** Worms, liver disorders
- **Cautions:** Unknown
- **Validity of Treatment:** Yes depending on cause of symptoms

32. **Bittersweet Nightshade** (Active ingredient is a steroidal alkaloid glycosin)

- **FP:** Skin irritations, bruising, rheumatism, nosebleeds
- **AS:** Rheumatism
- **Modern Use:** Cortisone-like effects, eczema, acne, warts
- **Cautions:** Pregnancy and lactation
- **Validity of Treatment:** Yes for skin disease & help rheumatic pain/swelling

33. **Blackberry** (Anthocyanins)

- **FP:** Diarrhea, kidney diseases, stomach ills
- **AS:** Diarrhea
- **Modern Use:** Astringent, diuretic, many chemo-preventative bioactivities
- **Cautions:** Unknown
- **Validity of Treatment:** Yes for diarrhea

34. **Black Pepper** (Piperine)

- **NA:** Arthritis, asthma, fever, cough, dysentery, dyspepsia, gas, skin damage
- **FP:** Scabies, stomach disorders
- **AS:** Menstrual headaches
- **Modern Use:** Antimicrobial, increases saliva & gastric juices, insecticidal effect, dysphagia, dyslipidemias
- **Cautions:** None
- **Validity of Treatment:** Yes for certain gastric illnesses

35. **Buckeye**

- **AS:** Rheumatism, if carried in pocket can cure colds and cramps
- **Modern Use:** No
- **Cautions:** None
- **Validity of Treatment:** No

36. **Burdoc** (Active ingredient is sulfur derivative)

- **FP:** Gout, rheumatism, dropsy, blood purifier, psoriasis
- **AS:** Scrofula TB, cramps
- **Modern Use:** Antibacterial, antifungal, diuretic, antioxidant, liver protectant, cancers
- **Cautions:** Unknown
- **Validity of Treatment:** Only against fungal or bacterial skin disorders.

37. **Calamus**

- **FP:** Digestive disorders, colic, fever
- **NA:** Worms, chew for toothache
- **AS:** Colic
- **Modern Use:** Stimulates appetite & digestion, sedative effect
- **Cautions:** Unknown
- **Validity of Treatment:** Yes gastric disorders

38. **Camphor** (Eugenol)

- **FP:** Body pain, skin problems, cold sores, arthritis, respiratory ills
- **AS:** Colds
- **NA:** Asthma, pain, heart problems
- **Modern Use:** Rheumatism, decrease Blood pressure, bronchitis, antispasmodic, antiseptic, heart arrhythmias, other bronchial disorders
- **Cautions:** Overdose in children, not for infants.
- **Validity of Treatment**: Yes

39. **Castor beans** (Active ingredient is ricin which is highly poisonous to the GI system)

- **AS:** General remedy, constipation, worms
- **NA:** Joint pain dyspepsia
- **Modern Use:** Laxative as castor oil
- **Cautions:** Highly poisonous, die in hypovolemic shock from severe GI bleeding, not for pregnant or under 12 years old
- **Validity of Treatment:** Yes to expel worms and for constipation

40. **Cinchona** (Active ingredient is quinine) quinine alkaloids

- **AS:** Malaria and other fevers
- **Modern Use:** Astringent and antiseptic, leg cramps
- **Cautions:** Unknown
- **Validity of Treatment:** Yes

41. **Corn poultice silk** (Active ingredient is saponin and tannins)

- **NA:** Sucks for boils, burns, inflammation, Tea for cold and flu
- **AS:** Silk resolves urinary problems, diuretic
- **Modern Use:** Stimulates cardiac muscle, increase blood pressure thus diuresis occurs, sedates GI tract
- **Cautions:** Unknown, could raise BP and cause arrhythmias
- **Validity of Treatment:** Perhaps because of diuresis

42. **Cotton seeds, bark, and root** (Active ingredient gossypal from the seed is toxic)

- **FP/NA:** Nausea, vomiting, headache, gonorrhea, expel afterbirth, cystitis, snake bite, dysentery, male contraceptive
- **AS:** Abortifacient
- **Modern Use:** Causes uterine contraction, promotes abortion, lowers sperm count
- **Cautions:** Eye blindness, male infertility with chronic use
- **Validity of Treatment:** Yes for abortion & male sterility

43. **Elderberry**

- **NA:** Fever, headache, inflammation, colds, flu, laxative, gout, rheumatism, syphilis
- **AS:** Bladder infection, fever, stop bleeding
- **Modern Use:** Hay fever, decrease flu symptoms
- **Cautions:** None
- **Validity of Treatment:** Yes for allergic hay fever symptoms, might help because of vitamins within the berry

44. **Fennel oil**

- **FP:** Toothache, colic, gas, indigestion
- **AS:** Chills, fevers, whooping cough
- **Modern Use:** Anti-inflammatory, antispasmodic, antibacterial, antifungal, decreases blood pressure, bronchial congestion, cough, indigestion

- **Cautions:** Diabetics need to monitor fluctuations in blood sugars
- **Validity of Treatment:** Yes

45. **Feverfew** (Active ingredient has Aspirin components) parthenolides

- **FP:** Fevers, migraines, gas, GI disorders, toothache, allergies
- **AS:** Fevers
- **Modern Use:** Migraines, antiplatelet, antitumor, mast cell inhibition, rheumatism, arthritis, vertigo, fever, toothache, many cancer chemo-preventive bioactivities
- **Cautions:** Not during pregnancy or lactation or young children
- **Validity of Treatment:** Yes

46. **Flax or linseed** (Richest source of omega 3 fatty acids and lignons)

- **AS:** Mild illness, stomach disorders
- **Modern Use:** Lower cholesterol, prevent blood clots, laxative, cough, urinary problems, Cancer fighting
- **Cautions:** Ileus, GI inflammation
- **Validity of Treatment:** Yes

47. **Black Haw** (Active ingredient salicin, a close compound to Aspirin)

- **FP:** Diarrhea, prevent miscarriages, decrease bleeding after childbirth, bronchitis, asthmas
- **AS:** Colds, purgative
- **Modern Use:** Astringent, spasmolytic
- **Cautions:** Unknown
- **Validity of Treatment:** Possibly

ENDNOTES

Part 1 . . . Health Problems in Early America

1. Dolan, Fitzpatrick, Herrmann, *Nursing in Society A Historical Perspective*. 15th Ed. (Philadelphia: W.B. Saunders, 1983), 107
2. Ibid., 127-132
3. Ibid., 132

Part 2 . . . History of American Hospitals

1. Rosenberg, Charles E., *The Care of Strangers: The Rise of America's Hospital System*. (New York: Basic Books Inc. 1987), 5
2. O'Connor, Robin, "American Hospital: The First 2 Years," *Journal of the American Hospital Association*. Jan.1, 1976. 4-6
3. Rosenberg, *The Care of Strangers*, 16-25
4. Salvaggion, John, *New Orleans Charity Hospital*. (New Orleans: Louisiana State University Press, 1992)
5. Rosenberg, *The Care of Strangers*, 112
6. Ibid.,113
7. Wilbur, C. Keith, *Revolutionary Medicine 1,700-1800* 2nd ed (Connecticut: The Globe Pequot Press, 1997), 48
8. Eichner, L.G. MD. *The Military Practice of Medicine during the Revolutionary War*. October 2003 meeting of the Tredyffrin East town History Club, p. 26, http://www.tehistory.org/hqda/pdf/v41/Volume41_N1_025.pdf
9. Ibid., 28
10. Rao, Gautham, "Sailors' Health and National Wealth: Marine Hospitals in the Early Republic," *Common-plow*, vol. 9, no. 1Oct, 2008.
11. Portsmouth History Commission. *Moments in History,* http://www.portsmouthva.gov/history/2002nov_dec.aspx

12. Naval Hospital Boston Historic District, National Park Service, http://www.nps.gov/nr/travel/maritime/nav.htm
13. Old Naval Hospital Organization, http://www.oldnavalhospital.org/History_Streitmatter. html
14. Ibid.
15. Rao, Gautham, "Sailors' Health and National Wealth: Marine Hospitals in the Early Republic."
16. Rao, Gautham, "Marine Hospital," Cry Wolf Project, Dept. of History, New Jersey Institute of Technology. http://crywolfproject.org/sites/degault/files/Marine%20Hospitals-crying%20wolf.pdf
17. National Library of Medicine, National Institute of Health, http://www.nlm.nih.gov/exhibition/phs_history/seamen.ht ml
18. Portsmouth History Commission. *Moments in History.*
19. Old Naval Hospital Organization, http://www.oldnavalhospital.org/History_Streitmatter.html
20. Naval Hospital Boston Historic District, National Park Service, http://www.nps.gov/nr/travel/maritime/nav.htm

Part 3 . . . Medicine During the American Revolution

1. Shryock, Richard Harrison, *Medicine and Society in America: 1660-1860.* (New York: New York University Press. 1960), 54
2. Wilbur, C. Keith, *Revolutionary Medicine 1700-1800.* 2nd ed. (Connecticut: The Globe Pequot Press, 1997), 9
3. Ibid., 10
4. Ibid., 10-11
5. Ibid., 30-37
6. Ibid., 31
7. Rush, Benjamin, "To the Officers in the Army of the United American States: Directions for Preserving the Health of Soldiers." (Published by Order of Board of War, 1777)
8. Ward, Harry George, *Washington's Enforcers: Policing the Continental Army.* (Illinois: Southern Illinois University Press; 2006), 121-122.
9. Jones, John M.D., "Plain, Concise, and Practical Remarks on the Treatment of Wounds and Fractures; To Which is

Added, an Appendix, On Camp and Military Hospitals."
(Philadelphia: Robert Bell in Third Street, 1776)
10. Wilbur, *Revolutionary Medicine*, 48-49.
11. Http://www.revolutionarywar101.com/ american-units/pa-02
12. Lang, Patrick (1939) "The Horrors of the English Prison ships, 1776-1783 and the Barbarous Treatment of the American patriots Imprisoned on Them," Society of the Friend, Sons of Saint Patrick.
13. Dring, Thomas, and Greene, Albert. *Recollections of the Jersey Prison Ship*. 2nd ed. (Westholme Publishing, 2010)
14. Taylor, George, *Martyrs to the Revolution in the British Prison Ships in the Wallabout Bay*. (Ulan Press, 2012, originally published in 1923)
15. Conversation with Maribeth and William Brannen (descendent of Dr. Welchel) of Alpharetta, Georgia concerning family history and Dr. Francis Welchel's medical treatment administered. Permission granted to include in manuscript.

Part 4 .... Antebellum Medicine

1. Buchan, William MD, (1790) Domestic Medicine: Or, A Treatise on the Prevention and cure of Disease by Regimen and Simple Medicines: With an Appendix, Containing a Dispensatory for the Use of Private Practitioners. (Edinburgh, Strahan, Balfour and Creech Publisher, Chapter IV. www.americanrevolution.org/ medicine. html.
2. Ibid. Chapter IV
3. Ibid. Chapter IV
4. Ibid. Chapter IX
5. Ibid., 121-122.
6. Rosenberg, Charles E, *The Care of Strangers: The Rise of America's Hospital* System, (New York: Basic Books Inc. 1987)
7. Shryock, *Medicine and Society in America.*
8. Wilbur, C. Keith, *Civil War Medicine 1861-1865* Illustrated Living History Series, (Connecticut: The Globe Pequot Press, 1998), 2

9   Stowe, Steven M., *Doctoring the South Southern Physicians and Everyday Medicine in the Mid-nineteenth Century*, (Chapel Hill: University of North Carolina, 2004), 152

10. Rutkow, Ira, *Seeking The Cure A History of Medicine in America*, (New York: Scribner Publishing, 2010)

Part 5 . . . The African Slave Healthcare System

1.   Rediker, Marcus, *The slave Ship A Human History*. (NewYork: Penguin group, 2007) p.5

2.   Thomas, Huge, *The Slave Trade The Story of the Atlantic Slave Trade 1440-1870*. New York: Simon and Schuster, 1997, 269-270

3.   Rediker, *The slave Ship A Human History*, 59

4.   Ibid., 274

5.   Kenny, Stephen C, "A Dictate of Both Interest and Mercy? Slave Hospitals in the Antebellum South." *Journal of the History of Medicine and Allied Sciences,* Volume 65, Number 1, 1-45

6.   "Civil Practice to Civil War," *The Medical College State of South Carolina 1861-65*, http://waring.library.musc.edu/exhibits/civilwar/index.php

7.   Waring, Joseph, *A History of Medicine in South Carolina 1825-1900*. (Charleston: South Carolina Medical Association, 1967), 135

8.   Historical Collections and Archives, Greenblatt Library Georgia Health Sciences University, Augusta, GA. http://www.gru.edu/library/greenblatt/archives/index.php

9.   Ibid.

10. Kenny, "A Dictate of Both Interest and Mercy," 28-30

11. Ibid., 31-45

12. Duffy, John ed., *The Rudolph Matas History of Medicine in Louisiana*. Vol. II, (Louisiana State University Press, 1962), 233

13. Leavitt, Judith & Numbers, Ronald ed., *Sickness &Health in American Readings in the History of Medicine and Public Health*. 3rd ed. (Madison: University of Wisconsin Press, 1997), 309-313.

14. Kenny, "A Dictate of Both Interest and Mercy," 24
15. Waring, *A History of Medicine in South Carolina*, 18-79
16. Kenny, "A Dictate of Both Interest and Mercy," 53-55
17. Stowe, Steven M, *Doctoring the South Southern Physicians and Everyday Medicine in the mid-nineteenth Century*, (Chapel Hill: University of North Carolina Press, 2004), 65
18. Lossing, Benson, *Pictorial Field book of the Revolution*. Vol. II, 1850, NY: Harper Brothers, 35
19. Blanton, Wyndham, *Medicine in Virginia in the Nineteenth Century*. (Richmond: Garrett & Massie, 1933), 71
20. Warner, John Harley, "A southern Medical Reform: The Meaning of the Antebellum Argument for Southern Medical Education," *Bulletin of the History of Medicine* 57, fall 1983, 365
21. Sims, J. Marion., *The Story of My Life*. (New York: Appleton and Co. 1884), 230-243 as quoted In Stephen Kenner's "Constructing the Slave Body," 58-60
22. Ibid., 58-60
23. Brown, John, *Slave Life in Georgia: A narrative of the Life, Sufferings, and Escape of John Brown, A Fugitive Slave*. (London: W.M. Watts. 1885, Reprinted with editing by F.N. Boney 1972 Savannah: Beehive Press), 45-48
24. Kolchin, Peter, *American Slavery 1619-1877*. 10th ed. (New York: Hill and Wang, 1993), 114
25. Pollett, Richard, *The Sugar Masters Planters, and Slaves in Louisiana's Cane World1820-1860*. (Baton Rouge: Louisiana University Press, 2005), 189-190
26. Blanton, *Medicine in Virginia in the Eighteenth Century*, 169
27. Ibid., 169
28. Clinton, Catherine, *The Plantation Mistress Woman's World in the Old South*. (NewYork: Pantheon Books, 1982)
29. Pavich-Lindsay, Melanie ed., *Anna The letters of St. Simons Island Plantation Mistress, 1817-1859*. (Athens: University of Georgia Press, 2002), xxix
30. Blanton, *Medicine in Virginia in the Eighteenth Century*, 169
31. Waring, *A History of Medicine in South Carolina*, 7-8
32. Ibid., 8

33. Ferguson, T. Reed, *The John Couper Family at Cannon's Point.* (Macon: Mercer University Press, 1994), 100-103
34. Ibid., 101
35. Vlach, John Michael, *Back of the Big House the Architecture of Plantation Slavery.* (Chapel Hill: University of North Carolina Press. 1993), 144
36. Ibid., 145
37. Marye, Florence, *The Story of The Page—King Family of Retreat Plantation, St Simons Island and of the Golden Isles of Georgia.* (Darien GA: Darien Printing & Graphics, 2000), 19-20
38. Butler, Scott, "Phase III Data Recovery Excavations at St. Annes Slave Settlement, Glynn County, Georgia," Brockington and Associates, Inc. Atlanta, 2005. Permission granted by Scott Butler, August 2012.

Part 6 . . . Basics of Negro Medicine

1. Kenny, Stephen C., "A Dictate of Both Interest and Mercy. Slave Hospitals in the Antebellum South." *Journal of the History of Medicine and Allied Sciences*, Volume 65.
2. Washington, Harriet A., *Medical Apartheid: The Dark History of Medical Experimentation on Black Americans from Colonial Times to the Present.* (New York, Anchor Books Division of Random House Inc. 2006)
3. Savitt, Todd L. *Medicine and Slavery The Diseases and Health Care of Blacks in Antebellum Virginia,* (Urbana and Chicago: University of Illinois Press, 2002)
4. Ibid., 14-16
5. Ibid., 36
6. Ibid., 34
7. Ibid., 35
8. Washington, *Medical Apartheid*, 36
9. Haller, John S, "The Physician versus the Negro: Medical and Anthropological Concepts of Race in the Late Nineteenth Century," *Bulletin of the History of Medicine,* 1970, no. 44: 251-252

10. Yandell LP., "Remarks on Struma Africana or the disease called Negro Poison or Negro Consumption" *Transylvania Journal of Medicine and Associated Sciences.* 1831 no 4: 83-103.

11. Berkow, Robert, Beers, Mark ed., *The Merck Manual of Medical Information.* (New Jersey: Merck Research laboratories Division of Merck and Co, Inc., 1997

12. Leavitt, Judith & Numbers, Ronald Ed., *Sickness & Health in America Readings in the History of Medicine and Public Health.* 3rd. ed. (Madison: University of Wisconsin Press, 1997), 352-354

13. Stead, William W. MD, "Genetics and Resistance to Tuberculosis Could Resistance be Enhanced by Genetic Engineering?" *Annals of Medicine.* The American College of Physicians, (1 June 1992) vol. 116 number 11, 937-939

14. Cartwright, Samuel MD, "Diseases and Peculiarities of the Negro Race." *DeBow's Review, Southern and Western States* (1851) Vol. XI, New Orleans: AMS Press Inc. 1967.

15. Savitt, *Medicine and Slavery,* 119-129

16. Stowe, Steven M., *Doctoring the South Southern Physician and Everyday Medicine in the mid-nineteenth Century.* (Chapel Hill: University of North Carolina Press, 2004), 211

17. Wilbur, C. Keith MD, *Civil War Medicine.* (Guildford, Conn: The Globe Pequot Press, 1998), 3-4

18. Smeltzer, Suzanne and Bare, Brenda G., *Brunner and Suddarth's Textbook of Medical Surgical Nursing* 10th ed., Vol. 1(Philadelphia: Lippincott Williams and Wilkins, 2004), 869-886

19. Wilson, John S., "The Negro" *American Cotton Planter and Soil of the South,* NS 2(Nov 1858) p 355, 3(Feb., March, June, July 1859) pp. 67-68,92,93,197,198, 228-229 as quoted in James D. Breedon: *Advice Among Masters: The Ideal in Slave Management in the Old South 1980,* (Westport Conn: Greenwood Press), 220

20. Ibid.

21. Stowe, Steven M., *Doctoring the South,* 4-5

22. Center for Disease Control: http://www.CDC.Gov

23. Washington. *Medical Apartheid,* 40-41

24. Leavitt, Judith & Numbers, Ronald Ed., *Sickness & Health in America Readings in the History of Medicine and Public Health*, 3rd. ed. (Madison: University of Wisconsin Press, 1997), 352-352

25. Smeltzer, *Textbook of Medical Surgical Nursing*. pp. 886-891

26. Berkow, *The Merck Manual*, 749-751, 898-900

27. World Health Organization, http://www.who.int/mediacenter

28. Berkow, *The Merck Manual*, 24

29. Schacter, Daniel; Gilbert, Daniel; Wegner, Daniel, "American Anthropological Association Statement on Race and Intelligence," *Psychology*, (New York: Worth Publishing, 2009)

30. Templeton, A. R., "The Genetic and Evolutionary Significance of Human Races." I*n: Race and Intelligence: Separating Science From Myth*. J. M. Fish, ed. pp. 31-56. (Mahwah, New Jersey, Lawrence Erlbaum Associates, 2002)

31. Beals, KL; Smith, CL; Dodd, SM, "Brain Size, Cranial Morphology, Climate, and Time Machines," *Current Anthropology* 25 (3): (June 1984): 301-30

32. Lieberman, Leonard, "How Caucasoids Got Such Big Crania and Why They Shrank: From Morton to Rushton," *Current Anthropology* 42: (February 2001), 69-95

33. Cernovsky, Z. Z., (1997), "A Critical Look at Intelligence Research," In Fox, D. & Prilleltensky, I. (Eds.) *Critical Psychology*, London: Sage, 121-133

34. *Journal of Blacks in Higher Education*, http://www.jbhe.com

35. Savitt, *Medicine and Slavery*, 38-41

36. Ibid., 39

37. Ibid., 40

38. Berkow, The Merck Manual, 885-891

39. Kasper and et. *Harrison's Manual of Medicine* 16th ed. (New York: McGraw-Hill Medical Publishing Division), 495-502

40. Manson-Bahr; Wilcocks, Charles, *Tropical Diseases*. 1966: London, 14

41. Savitt, *Medicine and Slavery*, 65-66

42. Washington, *Medical Apartheid*, 36-37

43. Haller, "The Physician Versus the Negro," 238-239

44. Washington, *Medical Apartheid*.

45. Berkow. *The Merck Manual*, 1215
46. Morais, *International Library of Negro Life and History*, 18
47. Leavitt, *Sickness & Health in America*, 356
48. Beckwith, J. Bruce, "The Sudden Infant Death Syndrome" *Current Problems in Pediatrics*, 3 (June 1973), 36-49
49. American SIDS Institute. http://www.SIDS.org
50. Leavitt, *Sickness & Health in America*, 355
51. Kasper, *Harrison's Manual of Medicine*, 485-486
52. Savitt, *Medicine and Slavery*, 60-61
53. American Lung Association, "Lung Disease Data in Culturally Diverse Communities," 2005
54. Centers for Disease control and Prevention, "Health Disparities Experienced by Black or African-Americans-United States" *MMWR,* Jan 14, 2005; vol. 54, 1-3

Part 7 . . . African Medicine of the 1800's

1. Yoder, D., *Folk Medicine Folklore and Folk Life: An Introduction*, (Chicago: University of Chicago Press 1972), 191-215
2. Kaippner, S. and Colodgin, B., "Folk Healing and Herbal Medicine: An Overview," *Folk Medicine and Herbal Healing*, (Illinois; Charles C. Thomas, 1981), 12-29
3. Covey, Herbert C., *African American Slave Medicine, Herbal and Non-herbal Treatments*. (New York: Lexington Books, 2007)
4. Ibid., 57-58.
5. Washington, Harriet A., *Medical Apartheid The Dark History of Medical Experimentation on Black Americans from Colonial Times to the Present*, (New York: Anchor Books, 2006), 50
6. Ibid., 51.
7. Leavitt, Judith Walzer and Numbers, Ronald L., *Sickness and Health in America, Readings in the History of Medicine and Public Health*, 3rd ed. (Madison, WI: University of Wisconsin, 199), 365
8. Minges, Patrick, *Black Indian Slave Narratives*, (North Carolina: John F. Blair Publishers, 2004)

9. Stowe, Steven M, *Doctoring the South: Southern Physicians and Everyday Medicine in the Mid-nineteenth Century*, (Chapel Hill: University of North Carolina Press, 2004), 134-135

10. Savitt, Todd L, *Medicine and Slavery: The Diseases and Health Care of the Blacks in Antebellum Virginia*, (Chicago: University of Chicago, 2002), 178

11. Shryock, Richard H, *Medicine and Society in America: 1660-1860*, (Ithaca NY: York University Cornell University Press, 1960), 27

12. Stowe, *Doctoring the South*, 156

13. Savitt, Todd L. *Race and Medicine in Nineteenth and Early twentieth Century America* (Kent, Ohio: Kent State University Press, 2007), 75

14. Savitt, Todd L, *Medicine and Slavery*, 179-180

15. Follett, Richard. *The Sugar Masters, Planters and Slaves in Louisiana's Cane World 1820-1860*, Baton Rouge: Louisiana State University Press, 2005), 188

16. Covey, Herbert C, *African American Slave Medicine*, 28

17. Ibid., 129-146

18. Ibid., 135

19. Ibid., 143

Part 8 . . . American Civil War Medicine 1861-1865

1. Freemon, Frank R, *Gangrene and Glory Medical Care During the American Civil War* (Chicago: University of Illinois Press, 2001)

2. Gillett, Mary C, *The Army Medical Department 1818-1865: Army Historical Series* (Washington D.C.: Center of Military History United States Army, 1987), 277

3. Ibid., 275

4. Woodward, Joseph Janvier, *Outlines of the Chief Camp Disease of The United States Armies as Observed During the Present War: A Practical Contribution to Military Medicine.* (Philadelphia: J.B. Lippincott & Co., 1863)

5. Ibid., 120-122

6. Freemon, Frank R, *Gangrene and Glory*, 212

7. Chisholm, Julian John, *A Manual of Military Surgery, For The Use of Surgeons in The confederate States Army; With explanatory Plates of All Useful Operations,*3rded. (Columbia: Evans and Cogswell, 1864), 246

8. Center for Disease Control and Prevention www.Nc.cdc.gov/eid/article/9/10/03-0287_aritcle.htm

9. Ibid.

10. Woodward, Joseph Janvier. *Outlines of the Chief Camp Disease,* 120-123

11. Goldsmith, M Dr., "A Report on Hospital Gangrene Erysipelas and Pyaemia as Observed in the Departments of the Ohio and the Cumberland" (Louisville: Bradley and Gilbert, 1863), 33

12. Chisholm, *A Manual of Military Surgery,* 240

13. Ibid., 243

14. Ibid., 24

15. Keen, William Williams, "Surgical Reminiscences of the Civil War," *Transactions of the College of Doctors of Philadelphia,* 3rd Series (1905): 27, 98-113

16. Chisholm, *A Manual of Military Surgery,* 409

17. "Soldier Life: Prisons and Hospitals," *The Photographic History of the Civil War,* Volume 4: (January 1,1987: Blue & Grey Press), 61.

18. Gillett, *The Army Medical Department*

19. Chisholm, *A Manual of Military Surgery*

20. Huntington, DL, "Anesthetics in the Civil War," *Barnes J I* ed., *The Medical and Surgical History of the War of the Rebellion,* Part III. (Washington DC: US War Dept. 1883)

21. Gillett, *The Army Medical Department,* 287

22. Long, Jim, *Herbal Medicines of the Civil War,* (Missouri: Long Creek Herbs Publisher, 2004), 9

23. Barnes, Joseph, *Medical and Surgical History of the War of the Rebellion* Vol. 3

24. Cunningham, H.H, *Doctors in Gray: The Confederate Medical Service,* (Baton Rouge: Louisiana State University Press, 1986)

25. Bollet, Alfred Jay, *Civil War Medicine: Challenges and Triumphs.* (Tucson, AZ: Galen Publishers, 2002)

26. Ibid.

27. *Medical and Surgical History of the War of the Rebellion 1861-1865* Part II, Vol. II, 677.
28. Chan, Chi-Chao, MD, *Sympathetic Ophthalmia*, January 2003, American Uveitis Society http://www.uveitissociety.org/pages/index.html.
29. Hughes, Michael O, "Eye Injuries and Prosthetic Restoration in the American Civil War Years," Journal of Ophthalmic Prosthetics http://www.artificialeyeclinic.com
30. Taylor, William H. MD, "Some Experiences of a Confederate Assistant Surgeon, *Transactions of the College of Physicians of Philadelphia.* 3rd series, Vol. 28, 1906, 91-121
31. Dammann, Gordon, DDS and Bollet, Alfred Jay MD, *Images of Civil war Medicine A Photographic History.* (New York: Demos Publishing, 2008), 27
32. Chisholm, *A Manual of Military Surgery*, 93
33. Donahue, M. Patricia PH.D., R.N. *Nursing The Finest Art An Illustrated History,* (St Louis: C.V. Mosby Co., 1985), 308
34. Goodnow, *Nursing History in Brief,* 17

Part 9 Revolutionary Advancements

1. Freemon, Frank R, *Gangrene and Glory: Medical Care During the American Civil* War (Chicago: University of Illinois Press, 2001), 75
2. Breeden, James, "Medicine at Antietam" *Caduceus: A Humanities Journal for the Medicine and Health Sciences* No. 1 (1994), 12
3. Letterman, Jonathan, *Medical Recollections of the Army of the Potomac* (Mass: Applewood Books, 1866)
4. Boffard, Kenneth D. *Manual of Definitive Surgical Trauma Care* 2nd ed., (London: Hodder Arnold, 2007), 18
5. Ibid., 173
6. Donahue, M. Patricia PH.D., R.N., *Nursing The Finest Art An Illustrated History,* (St. Louis: C.V. Mosby Co. 1985), 327-333
7. Ibid., 397-408
8. Health Resources and Services Administration Bureau of Health Professions National Center for Health Workforce Analysis April 2013, The U.S. Nursing Workforce: Trends in

Supply and Education http://bhpr.hrsa.gov/healthworkforce1/ reports/nursingworkforce, 5

9. Chisholm, Julian John, *A Manual of Military Surgery, For The Use of Surgeons in The confederate States Army; With explanatory Plates of All Useful Operations,* 3rd ed. (Columbia: Evans and Cogswell, 1864)

10. Hart, AG, *The Surgeon and the Hospital in the Civil War,* (Gaithersburg: Olde Soldeir Book, 1987)

11. Cunningham, H.H., *Doctors in Gray: The Confederate Medical Service,* (Baton Rouge: Louisiana State University Press, 1986)

12. *Medical and Surgical History of the War of the Rebellion 1861-1865* Vol. 1, 415-416.

13. Bollet, Alfred Jay, *Civil War Medicine: Challenges and Triumphs,* 168

14. Gross, Dr. Samuel David, *A Manual of Military Surgery* (Massachusetts: Applewood Books, 1861)

15. Cunningham, *Doctors in Gray,* 134.

16. Bollet, *Civil War Medicine,* 153

17. Ibid., 160

18. Wegner, Ansley Herring, *Phantom Pain North Carolina's Artificial Limbs Program for Confederate Veterans.* Raleigh, (North Carolina Dept. of Cultural Resources Office of Archives and History, 2004)

19. Bollet, *Civil War Medicine,* 174

20. Chisholm, *A Manual of Military Surgery,* 313

21. Ibid., 427

22. Duffard, *Manual of Definitive Surgical Trauma Care,* 175

23. Adams, George W, *Doctors in Blue The Medical History of the Union Army In the Civil War,* (Baton Rouge: Louisiana State University Press, 1980), 150

24. Ibid.

25. Cunningham, *Doctors in Gray,* 231

26. Adams, *Doctors in Blue,* 147.

27. Center for Disease Control, www.CDC.gov/handwashing

28. Bollet, *Civil War Medicine,* 44

29. Adams, *Doctors in Blue,* 3

30. National Museum of Health and Medicine, http://www.medicalmuseum.mil/index

31. Walter Reed National Medical and Military Center, www. wrnmmc.capmed.mil
32. Morais, Herbert, *International Library of Negro Life and History*, (New Year: Publishers Co. 1970), 36
33. Ibid., 49
34. Ibid., 50
35. Ibid., 40-49
36. Ibid., 70-71

Part 10 Epilogue

1. Oakes, James, *Slavery and Freedom* (New York: Norton and Co., 1990), 196
2. Johannsen and Venet ed., *The Union in Crisis Sources of the American Tradition*, (Massachusetts: Copley Publishing, 2003), 33
3. Du Bois, W.E.B., Black *Reconstruction in America 1860-1880*, (New York: Atheneum, 1972), 587
4. Ibid., 588

Appendix I

1. Castleman, Michael, *The Healing Herbs*, (New York: Bantam Books, 1995)
2. *PDR for Herbal Medicines* 4th Ed., (New Jersey: Thomson Healthcare Inc. 2007)
3. Covey, *African American Slave Medicine*, 1-194.
4. Long, Jim, *It will Do No Harm to Try It. The Home Remedies Diary of Elias Slagle 1859*, (Missouri: Long Creek Herbs Publisher, 2003)
5. Long, Jim, *Herbal Medicines of the Civil War*, (Missouri: Long Creek Herbs Publisher, 2004)
6. Collins,_*Practical Rules for the Management and Medical Treatment of Negro Slaves in The Sugar Colonies*, (London, and eGoogle books, 1803, www.archives.org, Blackett, R.J.M, 1986)

7. *Running a Thousand Miles for Freedom, The Escape of William and Ellen Craft From Slavery,* (Baton Rouge: Louisiana State University Press.)
8. Brown, John, *Slave Life in Georgia.* (Savannah: Beehive Press, 1972)
9. Duke, J. et al, *CRC Handbook of Medicinal Spices,* (Boca Raton: CRC Press, 2003)
10. Ulbricht and Seamon eds., *Natural Standard Herbal Pharmacotherapy: An Evidenced-Based Approach,* (St Louis: Mosby Elsevier, 2010)
11. Foster, S. Johnson, R.L., *National Geographic Desk Reference to Nature's Medicine,* (Washington DC: National Geographic Society, 2006)

GLOSSARY

Sources: New Oxford Dictionary (www.oxforddictionary.com) and Center for Disease Control (www.CDC.gov)

Almshouse: Charitable housing provided to enable people (typically elderly people who can no longer work to earn enough to pay rent) to live in a particular community.

Amputation: The surgical removal of a body extremity as a result of disease or injury.

Analgesic: A painkiller drug used to provide relief from pain that acts on peripheral or central nervous systems.

Antiseptic: Substance that prevents the growth of disease-causing organisms

Apothecary: A medical professional who formulates and dispenses drugs to physicians, surgeons and patients; a role now served by a pharmacist.

Bloodletting: The withdrawal of small quantities of blood from a patient to cure or prevent illness or disease.

Botulism: Food poisoning caused by a bacteria growing in improperly cooked or canned foods, sometimes fatal to humans.

Brain abscess: An abscess in the brain caused by inflammation and collection of infectious material.

Cadaver: A corpse is called a cadaver when it is intended for dissection.

Cholera: An infectious and often fatal bacterial disease of the small intestine, typically contracted from infected water supplies and causing severe vomiting and diarrhea.

Compound fracture: An injury in which a broken bone pierces the skin, causing a risk of infection.

Contagious: A disease spread through contact with the object or person (infectious).

Contrabands: During the American Civil War, Confederate-owned slaves who sought refuge in Union military camps or who lived in territories that fell under Union control were declared "contraband of war". Term first articulated by Gen. Benjamin Butler in 1861.

Convalescent: A person who is recovering after an illness or operation. Convalescence is a later stage of infectious disease when patient is recovering but may continue to be a source of infection.

Cupping: A therapy in which heated glass cups are applied to the skin along the meridians of the body, creating suction as a way of stimulating the flow of energy.

Diphtheria: An acute, highly-contagious bacterial disease causing inflammation of the mucous membranes, formation of a false membrane in the throat that hinders breathing and swallowing, and potentially fatal heart and nerve damage by a bacterial toxin in the blood.

Disinfectant: A chemical liquid that destroys bacteria.

Dispensary: A medical clinic provided by charitable or public funds.

Dura mater: The tough outermost membrane enveloping the brain and spinal cord.

Dysentery: Infection of the intestines, especially the colon, resulting in severe diarrhea with the presence of blood and mucus in the feces, known as bloody flux.

Endemic: A disease regularly or continuously found among people in a certain area, coastal South for instance.

Epidemic: A disease that is continually present in an area and affects a relatively small number of people.

Gangrene: Localized death and decomposition of body tissue, resulting from either obstructed circulation or bacterial infection and potentially life threatening.

Gas gangrene: Rapidly spreading gangrene occurring in dirty wounds infected by bacteria that gives off a foul-smelling gas. This disease is usually caused by anaerobic Clostridium bacteria.

Heat stroke: Heat stroke is a heat illness defined as a body temperature of greater than 40.6 °C (105.1 °F) due to environmental heat exposure with impairment of the body's thermoregulation.

Herb: Any plant with leaves, seeds, or flowers used for flavoring, food, medicine, or perfume.

Heroic medicine: Heroic medicine therapies are the aggressive medical practices or methods of treatment used until the mid-nineteenth century, particularly the dangerous and unproven treatments that scientific advances later replaced.

Hypoxia: A pathological condition in which the body or a region of the body is deprived of an adequate oxygen supply.

Impetigo: A contagious bacterial skin infection forming pustules and yellow, crusty sores and caused by the bacteria Streptococcus pyogenes or S. aureus.

Infectious: A disease that is spread via microorganisms in the air or water. (contagious)

Infirmary (slave): A small place within a hospital or separate facility that cares only for free blacks or slaves.

Inflammation: Inflammation is a protective attempt by the organism to remove the injurious stimuli and to initiate the healing process. Inflammation is not a synonym for infection. The classical signs of acute inflammation are pain, heat, redness, swelling, and loss of that body part's function.

Inoculation: Inoculation is a method of purposefully infecting a person (with smallpox) in a controlled manner so as to minimize the severity of the infection and also to induce immunity against further infection.

Jaundice: A medical condition with yellowing of the skin or whites of the eyes, arising from excess of the pigment bilirubin and typically caused by obstruction of the bile duct, by liver disease, or by excessive breakdown of red blood cells.

Meningitis: Acute inflammation of the protective membranes covering the brain and spinal cord.

Miasma: An oppressive or unpleasant atmosphere that surrounds or a smell that emanates from something.

Necrosis: The death of most or all of the cells in an organ or tissue due to disease, injury, or failure of the blood supply.

Necrotic enteritis: Inflammation and then death of the intestine, esp. the small intestine, usually accompanied by diarrhea, caused by clostridium bacteria.

Negro medicine: A Southern specialty of treating Negro slaves in the Old South by doctors, who theorize the differences of races result in different methods of medical care.

Ophthalmic: Relating to the eye and its diseases.

Pest house: A hospital for people who may have or show signs of an infectious disease.

Pneumonia: A lung inflammation caused by bacterial or viral infection, in which the air sacs fill with pus.

Prosthesis: An artificial body part.

Puking: Vomiting.

Pulmonary: Pertaining to the lungs.

Pus: A thick yellowish or greenish opaque liquid produced in infected tissue, consisting of dead white blood cells and bacteria with tissue debris and serum.

Quarantine: A place of isolation or separation in which people or animals that have arrived from elsewhere or been exposed to infectious or contagious disease are placed.

Resection (bone): A surgical procedure to cut out a small piece of tissue such as bone.

Rheumatic arthritis: A painful inflammation and stiffness of the joints. An autoimmune disease that results in a chronic, systemic inflammatory disorder that may affect many tissues and organs, but principally attacks flexible joints.

Scarlet fever: An infectious bacterial disease affecting mostly children and causes fever and a scarlet rash. It is caused by streptococci.

Septic arthritis: The purulent invasion of a joint by an infectious agent, which produces arthritis.

Septicemia: Blood poisoning, when bacteria or their toxins spreads throughout the bloodstream resulting in septic shock if left untreated.

Sick house: Plantation hospital where slaves were treated for injury or illness by slave nurses in the Old South.

Sickle-cell Disease: A hereditary blood disorder, characterized by red blood cells that assume an abnormal, rigid, sickle shape. Sickle-cell disease occurs more commonly among people whose ancestors lived in tropical and sub-tropical sub-Saharan regions where malaria is or was common.

SIDS: Sudden infant death syndrome is marked by the sudden death of an infant that is not predicted by medical history. The death remains unexplained after a thorough forensic autopsy and detailed death scene investigation. As infants are at the highest risk for SIDS during sleep, it is sometimes referred to as cot death or crib death.

Tetanus: A bacterial disease marked by rigidity and spasms of the voluntary muscles caused by *Clostridium Tetani.*

Trepanning: Making a burr hole, a surgical intervention in which a hole is drilled or scraped into the human skull, exposing the dura mater to treat health problems related to intracranial diseases.

Typhoid fever: An infectious bacterial fever with an eruption of red spots on the chest and abdomen and severe intestinal irritation and caused by Salmonella typhi.

Typhus: An infectious disease caused by rickettsia and characterized by a purple rash, headaches, fever, and usually delirium, and historically a cause of high mortality during wars and famines. There are several forms transmitted by vectors such as lice, ticks, mites, and rat fleas. (Also called spotted fever.)

Vaccinate: Administration of antigenic material (a vaccine) to stimulate an individual's immune system to develop adaptive immunity to a pathogen. Vaccines can prevent or ameliorate morbidity from infection.

Vesico-vagina fistula: An abnormal fistulous tract extending between the bladder (or vesico) and the vagina that allows the continuous involuntary discharge of urine into the vaginal vault.

Yellow fever: A tropical viral disease affecting the liver and kidneys, causing fever and jaundice and is often fatal. It is transmitted by mosquitoes and known historically as Yellow Jack is an acute viral hemorrhagic disease

Bibliography

Books and Journals

Alcott, Louisa May. *Civil War Hospital Sketches*. New York: Dover Publications Inc., 2006.

Adams, George W. *Doctors In Blue: The Medical History Of The Union Army In The Civil War*. Baton Rouge: Louisiana State University press, 1980.

Barnes, Joseph. *Medical And Surgical History of the War Of The Rebellion*, Vol. 3 Washington Government printing office, 1883.

Beales, KL; Smith, CL; Dodd SM. "Brain size, Cranial Morphology, Climate, Time Machines," *Current Anthropology*, June 1984.

Berkow, Robert; Beers, Mark ed. *The Merck Manual Of Medical Information*. New Jersey; Merck research laboratories division of Merck and Company Inc., 1997.

Bracket, RJM. *Running A Thousand Miles For Freedom, The Escape Of William and Ellen Craft From Slavery*. Baton Rouge: Louisiana State University Press, 1986.

Blanton, Wyndham. *Medicine In Virginia In The 19th Century*. Richmond: Garrett and Massey, 1933.

Boffard, Kenneth D. *Manual Of Definitive Surgical Trauma Care*. 2nd ed. London: Hodder Arnold, 2007.

Bollet, Alfred J. *Civil War Medicine: Challenges and Triumphs*. Tucson, AZ: Galen Publishers, 2002.

Breeden, James. "Medicine At Antietam," *Caduceus: Inhumanity Journal For The Medicine And Health Sciences* No. 1. 1994.

Brown, John. *Slave Life in Georgia: A Narrative Of The Life, Sufferings, And Escape Of John Brown, A Fugitive Slave.* London: W Sam Watts 1855 (reprinted with editing by F.N. Boney) Savannah Beehive Press, 1972.

Butler, Scott. "Phase III Data Recovery Excavations At St. Anne's Slave Settlement, Glynn County, Georgia." Atlanta: Brockington and Associates, Inc. 2005.

Cartright, Samuel MD. "Diseases And Peculiarities of the Negro Race." *Dubose Review Southern And Western States* 1851Vol.XI, New Orleans: AMD Press Inc. 1967.

Castleman, Michael. *The Healing Herbs.* New York: Bantam books 1995.

Centers for Disease Control and Prevention "Health Disparities Experienced By Black or African Americans United States." *MWR,* CDC, January 14, 2005.

Chernosky, Z.Z. "A Critical Look At Intelligence Research," In Fox, D and Prilleltensky I. *Critical Psychology.* London: Sage, 1997.

Chisholm, Julian John. *A Manual Of Military Surgery For The Use of Surgeons In The Confederate States Army: With Explanatory Plates Of All Useful Operations,* 3rd edition. Columbia: Evans and Cogswell, 1864.

Clinton, Catherine. *The Plantation Mistress Woman's World In The Old South.* New York: Pantheon Books, 1982.

Covey, Herbert. *African-American Slave Medicine, Verbal And Nonverbal Treatments.* New York: Lexington Books, 2007.

Cunningham, H. H. *Doctors In Gray: The Confederate Medical Service.* Baton Rouge: Louisiana State University Press, 1986.

Davis, William C. *The Battle Of New Market.* Baton Rouge: Louisiana State University Press, 1975.

Dammann, Gordon, DDS and Bollet, Alfred J MD. *Images Of Civil War Medicine* A *Photographic History.* New York: Demos Publishing, 2008.

Dolan, Fitzpatrick, Hermann. *Nursing In Society A Historical Perspective* 15th edition. Philadelphia: W. B. Saunders, 1983.

Donahue, M. Patricia PhD, RN. *Nursing The Finest Art An Illustrated History.* St. Louis: CV Mosby Company, 1985.

Dring, Thomas and Green, Albert. *Recollections Of The Jersey Prison Ship* 2nd ed., Westholme Publishing, 2010.

Du Bois WEB, "Black Reconstruction In America 1860-1880." New York: Athenaeum 1972.

Duke, J. et al, *CRC Handbook of Medicinal Spices*, Boca Raton: CRC Press, 2003.

Duffy, John editor. *The Rudolph Matas History Of Medicine In Louisiana.* Vol II, Louisiana State University Press, 1962.

Faust, Drew Gilpin. *This Republic Of Suffering: Death And The American Civil War.* New York: Vintage Books, 2008.

Ferguson, T. Reed. *The John Cooper Family At Cannon's Point.* Macon: Mercer University Press, 1994.

Follet, Richard. *The Sugar Masters, Planters, And Slaves In Louisiana Cane World 1822 1860.* Baton Rouge: Louisiana State University Press, 2005.

Foster, S. Johnson, R.L. *National Geographic Desk Reference to Nature's Medicine*. Washington DC: National Geographic Society, 2006.

Freemon, Frank R. *Gangrene and Glory: Medical Care During The American Civil War*. Chicago: University of Illinois Press, 2001.

Gillett, Mary. *The Army Medical Department 1818-1865: Army Historical Series*. Washington D.C: Center of Military History United States Army, 1987.

Goldsmith, M. Dr. *A Report On Hospital Gangrene Erysipelas And Pyema As Observed In The Departments Of The Ohio And Cumberland*. Louisville: Bradley and Gilbert, 1863.

Goodnow, Minnie RN. *Nursing History In Brief*. Philadelphia: WB Saunders Company, 1941.

Gross, Dr. Samuel David. *A Manual Of Military Surgery*. Massachusetts: Applewood Books, 1861.

Haller, John S. "The Doctors Versus The Negro: Medical And Anthropological Concepts Of Race In The Late 19th Century." *Bulletin of the History of Medicine*, 1970.

Hart, AG. *The Surgeon And The Hospital In The Civil War*. Gaithersburg: Olde Soldeir book, 1987.

Horton, James Oliver and Horton Louise E. *Slavery And The Making Of America*, New York: Oxford University Press, 2005.

Huntington, DL, and Otis GA. "Anesthetics In The Civil War." Barnes JT editor, *The Medical And Surgical History Of The War Of The Rebellion Part III*, Washington DC: US War Department, 1883.

Johannsen and Benet ed. *The Union In Crisis Sources of The American Tradition*. Massachusetts: Copley Publishing, 2003.

Johnson, Curt. *Battles of the American Revolution.* New York: Bonanza Books, 1984.

Jones, John MD. *Plain Concise And Practical Remarks On The Treatment Of Wounds And Fractures: To Which Is Added, An Appendix On Camp And Military Hospitals.* Philadelphia: Robert now in Third Street, 1776.

Kaippner, S. and Colodgin, B. "Folk Healing And Herbal Medicine: An Overview." Folk Medicine And Herbal Healing, Illinois: Charles C. Thomas, 1981.

Kasper and et. *Harrison's Manual Of Medicine* 16th ed. New York: McGraw—Hill Medical Publishing Division, 2005.

Keen, William Williams. "Surgical Reminiscences Of The Civil War," *Transactions of the College of Doctors.* Philadelphia, 3rd series, 1905.

Kenny, Stephen C. "A Dictate Of Both Interest And Mercy? Slave Hospitals In The Antebellum South." *Journal Of The History Of Medicine And Allied Services,* Vol. 65, No. 1.

Knight, Charles R. *Valley Thunder: The Battle of New Market And The Opening Of The Shenandoah Valley Campaign May 1864.* New York: Sanas Beatie, 2010.

Kolchin, Peter. *American Slavery 1619 to 1877* 10th ed. New York: Hill and Wang, 1993.

Lane, Patrick. *The Horrors Of The English Prison Ships, 1776-1783 And The Barbarous Treatment Of The American Patriots Imprisoned On Them,* Society of the Friendly Sons of Saint Patrick, 1939.

Leavitt, Judith and Numbers, Ronald ed. *Sickness And Health In America Readings In The History Of Medicine And Public Health,* 3rd ed. Madison: University of Wisconsin Press, 1997.

Letterman, Jonathan MD., *Medical Recollections Of The Army of Potomac*. Massachusetts: Applewood Books, 1866.

Lieberman, Leonard. "How Caucasoids Got Such Big Cranium And Why They Shrank: From Morton to Rushton," *Current Anthropology* 42: February 2001.

Long, Jim., *Herbal Medicines of The Civil War*. Missouri: Long Creek Herbs Publisher 2004.

Long, Jim., *It Will Do No Harm To Try It. The Home Remedies Diary of Elias Slagle 1859*. Missouri: Long Creek Herbs Publisher, 2003.

Lossing, Benson., *Pictorial Field Book Of The Revolution* Vol. II. New York: Harper's brothers, 1850. Wilcocks, Charles. *Tropical Diseases*. London: Manson-Bahr, 1966.

Marye, Florence., *The Story of The Page—King Family Of Retreat Plantation, St. Simons Island And of The Golden Isles of Georgia*. Darien Georgia: Darien Printing and Graphics, 2000.

Medical Surgical History of The War of The Rebellion 1861 to 1865 Vol. I. US Government Printing Office, 1870.

Minges, Patrick. *Black Indian Slave Narratives*. North Carolina: John F Blair Publishers, 2004.

Morais, Herbert. *International Library Of Negro Life And History, The History Of The Negro In Medicine*. 3rd edition, New York: Publishers Company, Inc. 1970.

Nightingale, Florence. *Notes On Hospitals 1859*. London; John W. Parker and Son reprinted by an ARUP, 2010.

Nightingale, Florence. *Notes On Nursing*. New York: Dover Publications, 1969.

Florence Nightingale Museum Booklet. London. Florence Nightingale Museum at St. Thomas Hospital. July 30, 1890.

Norris, David A. *Life During The Civil War.* Canada: History Magazine, 2009.

Nuland, Sherwin B. *Doctors: The Biography Of Medicine.* New York: Alfred A Knopf, 1988.

Oaks, James. *Slavery And Freedom.* New York: Norton and Company, 1999.

O'Connor, Robin. "American Hospital: The First 200 Years," *Journal of the American Hospital Association,* January 1, 1976.

Pasteur, Louis and Lister, Joseph. *Collected Writings.* New York; Kaplan Publishing, 2008.

Pavich-Lindsay, Melanie ed. *Anna The Letters of St Simons Island Plantation Mistress. 1817-1859,* Athens: University of GA Press, Athens, 2002.

PDR For Herbal Medicines 4th ed. New Jersey: Thomson Healthcare Inc., 2007.

Pollett, Richard. *The Sugar Masters, Planters, and Slaves in Louisiana's Cane World 1820 1860.* Baton Rouge: Louisiana University Press, 2005.

Porter, Roy. *Blood And Guts: A Short History Of Medicine.* New York: Norton Co. 2002.

Rao, Gautham. "Sailors Health And National Wealth: Marine Hospitals In The Early Republic," *Common—plow,* Vol. 9 No 1 October 2008.

Raphael, Ray. *A People's History of The American Revolution: How Common People Shaped The Fight For Independence*, New York: Perennial, 2001.

Rediker, Marcus. *The Slave Ship In Human History*. New York: Penguin Group 2007.

Reimer, Terry. *Divided By Conflict, United By Compassion*. Frederick Maryland: The NMCWM Press, 2004.

Rosenberg, Charles E, *The Care of Strangers: The Rise Of America's Hospital System*. New York: Basic Books Inc. 1987.

Rush, Benjamin., *To The Officers In The Army Of United American States: Directions For Preserving The Health Of Soldiers*, (Booklet) Published by Order of Board of War 1777.

Salvaggion, John., *New Orleans Charity Hospital*. New Orleans: Louisiana State University Press, 1992.

Savitt, Todd L., *Medicine and Slavery The Diseases and Health Care of Blacks in Antebellum Virginia*. Urbana and Chicago: University of Illinois Press, 2002.

Savitt, Todd L., *Race and Medicine in Nineteenth and Early twentieth Century America*. Kent, Ohio: Kent State University Press, 2007.

Schacter, Daniel; Gilbert, Daniel; Wegner, Daniel. "American Anthropological Association Statement on Race and Intelligence," *Psychology*. New York: Worth Publishing, 2009.

Schmidt, James and Hasegawa, Guy R. *Years of Change and Suffering: Modern Perspectives On Civil War Medicine*. Minnesota: Edinborough Press, 2009.

Shryock, Richard Harrison., *Medicine and Society in America: 1660-1860*. New York: New York University Press, 1960.

Sims, J. Marion., *The Story of My Life. New York: Appleton and Co. 1884* as quoted In Stephen Kenner's "Constructing the Slave Body."

Smeltzer, Suzanne and Bare. Brenda G. *Brunner and Suddarth's Textbook of Medical Surgical Nursing.* 10th ed. Vol. 1 Philadelphia: Lippincott Williams and Wilkins, 2004.

Stead, William W. MD, "Genetics and Resistance to Tuberculosis Could Resistance be Enhanced by Genetic Engineering?" *Annals of Medicine* by the American College of Doctors, Vol. 116, No. 11. 1 June 1992.

Stowe, Steven M., *Doctoring the South Southern Doctors and Everyday Medicine in the Mid-nineteenth Century.* Chapel Hill: University of North Carolina Press, 2004.

Swearingen, Pamela and Keen, Janet, *Manual of Critical Care Nursing Interventions and Collaborative Management* 4th ed. Missouri: Mosby Co., 2001.

Taylor, George, "Martyrs to the Revolution in the British Prison Ships in the Wallabout Bay" Ulan Press, 2012, originally published in 1923.

Taylor, William H. MD, "Some Experiences of a Confederate Assistant Surgeon," *Transactions of the College of Physicians of Philadelphia* 3rd series, Vol. 28, 1906.

Templeton, A. R. "The Genetic and Evolutionary Significance of Human Races." In: *Race and Intelligence: Separating Science From Myth.* J. M. Fish, ed. Mahwah, New Jersey, Lawrence Erlbaum Associates, 2002.

Thacher, James MD, *Eyewitness To The American Revolution: The Battles And Generals As seen By An Army Surgeon.* New York: Longmeadow Press, 1994.

Miller, Francis Trevelyan Ed, *The Photographic History of the Civil War*, Volume 4: Soldier Life; Prisons and Hospitals, Blue & Grey Press, 1987.

Thomas, Huge, *The Slave Trade The Story of the Atlantic Slave Trade 1440-1870*. New York: Simon and Schuster, 1997.

Turner, Edward, Raymond, *The New Market Campaign May 1864*. Richmond: New Market Battlefield Military Museum. Originally published by Whittet and Shepperson 1912.

Ulbricht and Seamon eds., *Natural Standard Herbal Pharmacotherapy: An Evidenced-Based Approach*. St Louis: Mosby Elsevier, 2010.

Vlach, John Michael, *Back of the Big House the Architecture of Plantation Slavery*. Chapel Hill: University of North Carolina Press, 1993.

Ward, Harry, *George Washington's Enforcers: Policing the Continental Army*. Illinois: Southern Illinois University Press, 2006.

Waring, Joseph, *A History of Medicine in South Carolina 1825-1900*. Charleston: South Carolina Medical Association, 1967.

Warner, John Harley, "A southern Medical Reform: The Meaning of the Antebellum Argument for Southern Medical Education," *Bulletin of the History of Medicine* 57, fall 1983.

Washington, Harriet A. *Medical Apartheid: The Dark History of Medical Experimentation on Black Americans from Colonial Times to the Present*. New York, Anchor Books Division of Random House Inc., 2006.

Wegner, Ansley Herring, *Phantom Pain North Carolina's Artificial Limbs Program For Confederate Veterans*. Raleigh, North Carolina Dept. of Cultural Resources Office of Archives and History, 2004.

Wilbur, C. Keith, *Civil War Medicine 1861-1865 Illustrated Living History Series*. Connecticut: The Globe Pequot Press, 1998.

Wilbur, C. Keith, *Revolutionary Medicine 1700-1800*, 2nd ed. Connecticut: The Globe Pequot Press, 1997.

Wilson, John S, "The Negro" *American Cotton Planter and Soil of the South*, NS 2(Nov 1858) 3(Feb., March, June, July 1859) as quoted in James D. Breedon: *Advice Among Masters: The Ideal in Slave Management in the Old South 1980*. Westport Conn: Greenwood Press.

Woodward, Joseph Janvier, *Outlines of the Chief Camp Disease of The United States Armies as Observed During the Present War: A Practical Contribution to Military Medicine*. Philadelphia: J.B. Lippincott & Co., 1863.

Yandell LP. 1831 "Remarks on Struma Africana or the disease called Negro Poison or Negro Consumption." *Transylvania Journal of Medicine and Associated Sciences*. No. 4.

Yoder, D. (1972) "Folk Medicine." *Folklore and Folk Life: An Introduction*, Chicago: University of Chicago Press, 1972.

Websites

American lung Association, Lung Disease Data in Culturally Diverse Communities. http:// www.lungusa.org/asseets/documents/publications/lung-disease data/LDD_2008.pdf

Collins, *Practical Rules for the Management and Medical Treatment of Negro Slaves in The Sugar Colonies*, London, and eGoogle books, 1803, www.archives.org, Blackett, R.J.M, 1986.

Buchan, William MD (1790) *Domestic Medicine: Or, A Treatise on the Prevention and* cure of Disease by Regimen and Simple Medicines: With an Appendix, Containing a Dispensatory for the Use of Private

Practitioners. (Edinburgh, Strahan, Balfour and Creech publishers), Chapter IV, www.americanrevolution.org/medicine.

Cantrell, LTC Nancy Bullard, Army Nurse Corps Historian, http:// history.amedd,army.mil/ ANCwebsite/about.html.

Center for Disease Control and Prevention. http://wwwnc.cdc.gov/eid/ article/ 9/10/03-0287_article.htm.

Chan, Chi-Chao, MD *Sympathetic Ophthalmia*, January 2003, American Uveitis Society, http://www.uveitissociety.org/pages/disease/ so.htm.

Civil Practice to Civil War, The Medical College State of South Carolina 1861-65, http:// waring.library.musc.edu/exhibits/civilwar/ index.php.

Eichner, L.G. MD, *The Military Practice of Medicine during the Revolutionary War*, October 2003 meeting of the Tredyffrin East town History Club, p. 26, http://www.tehistory.org/hqda/pdf/v41/ volume41_N1_025.pdf.

Health Resources and Services Administration Bureau of Health Professions National Center for Health Workforce Analysis April 2013, The U.S. Nursing Workforce: Trends in Supply & Education, http://bhpr.hrsa.gov/healthworkforce1/reports nursingworkforce/ nursingworkforce fullreport.pdf

Historical Collections and Archives, Greenblatt Library Georgia Health Sciences University, Augusta, GA. http://www.lib. georgiahealth.edu/archives/index.php.

Hughes, Michael O. "Eye Injuries and Prosthetic Restoration in the American Civil War Years," *Journal of Ophthalmic Prosthetics*, www. artificialeyeclinic.com/hughesarticle_ 2008 pdf. http://www.blnz. com/news/2008/04/23/seamens_sanctuary_marine_hospital_ service_2706.html.

Journal of Blacks in Higher Education, http://www.jbhe.com.

National Library of Medicine, National Institute of Health, http://www.nlm.nih.gov/exhibition/phs_history/seamen.html.

National Museum of Health and Medicine, http://www.medicalmuseum.mil/index.

Naval Hospital Boston Historic District, National Park Service, http://www.nps.gov/nr/travel/maritime/nav.htm.

Old Naval Hospital Organization, http://www.oldnavalhospital.org/historystreitmatter.html

Portsmouth History Commission, Moments in History, http://www.portsmouthva.gov/history/2002nov_dec.aspx.

Rao, Gautham, Marine Hospitals, Cry Wolf Project, Dept. of History, New Jersey Institute of Technology, http://crywolfproject.org/sites/default/files/Marine%20Hospitals-crying%20wolf.pdf.

Rao, Gautham, Sailors' Health and National Wealth: Marine Hospitals in the Early Republic, US Marine Hospital on line, http://www.marinehospital.org/post.html.

Walter Reed National Medical and Military Center, www.wrnmmc.capmed

Other Resources

Battlefield Parks, Museums, and Libraries,

    National Museum of Civil War Medicine Museum, Frederick, MD
    National Museum of Health and Medicine, Silver Spring, MD
    National Civil War Naval Museum, Port Columbus, GA
    Museum of the Confederacy, Richmond, VA
    Chimborazo Medical Museum, Richmond, VA

Massanutten Regional Library—Massanutten Regional Library, Harrisonburg, VA.
Handley Regional Library's Stewart Bell Jr. Archive, Winchester, VA
Virginia Military Institute, Lexington, VA.
Front Royal-Warren Rifles Confederate Museum of Front Royal, VA
Marietta Museum, Marietta, GA
Atlanta Historical Society, Atlanta, GA
Andersonville National Cemetery, Americus, GA
Cyclorama, Atlanta, GA
Georgia Historical Society, Savannah, GA.
Gettysburg National Battlefield Park, PA
Gettysburg Museum, PA
New Market Battlefield Park, VA.
Kennesaw National Battlefield, VA
Manassas National Battlefield Park, VA
Harpers Ferry National Park, WV
National Battlefield Winchester City, VA
Monocacy National Battlefield Park, MD
Antietam National Battlefield Park, MD
Stones River National Battlefield Park, VA
Franklin Tennessee National Battlefield Park, TN
Mildred Huie Museum, St. Simons Island, GA
Fort Frederica National Monument, St. Simons Island, GA
Valley Forge National Park and Museum, PA
Fort Washington Park, NY
Fort Lee museum, NJ
West Point, NY
Hudson River Highlands, NY

Historic towns/places:

Augusta, Roswell, Atlanta, Savannah, St. Simon's Island, Darien, GA
Charleston, SC
Frederick, MD
Richmond, Front Royal, Kernstown, Lexington, Fishers Hill, Staunton, Harrisonburg, Winchester, Berryville, George Washington's Home, Mt. Vernon, Winchester National Cemetery, VA

Franklin, Spring Hill, Nashville, Murfreesboro, Brentwood, Chattanooga, TN, McGavock Confederate Cemetery, Franklin, TN
Valley Forge, Philadelphia, PA
Elmsworth Cemetery, Sheperdstown, WV
Oakland Cemetery, Atlanta, Magnolia Cemetery, Augusta, Confederate Cemetery Marietta, GA

Journals and Newsletters:

The Journal of Civil War Medicine, The Official quarterly Publication of the Society of Civil War Surgeons
The Museum of the Confederacy Magazines
National Museum of Civil War Medicine Surgeons Call (Newsletters)
Civil War Trust Hallowed Ground (Newsletters)

INDEX

prison infirmaries, 11, 12
private, 10, 58, 125
public, 9
regimental, 15
religious, 158
sick houses, 16, 48, 64, 69, 73,
    74, 124, 163
slave hospital, 49, 114
slave infirmary, 49, 51, 52, 56
specialized, 10

M

medical care
African folk practitioners, 109
Medical care
spiritualists, 109
medical treatments, 16
bloodletting, 24, 25, 43, 53, 82,
    87, 115
cupping, 23, 43, 115
heroic medicine, 217
laudable pus, 25, 134
poultices, 27, 117, 136, 196
puking, 53, 69
purging, 23, 25, 42, 53, 69
medications
arsenic, 42
calomel, 70
caustic, 23, 24, 42, 53, 81, 82,
    115
ipecac, 42, 70
mercury, 23, 42, 149
medicine
Negro, 16, 49, 53, 62, 63, 66, 69,
    76, 79, 81, 83, 85, 87, 91, 94,
    124, 163, 218
mortality
infant, 86

N

nurse
Florence Nightingale, 40, 162,
    174, 228, 229
male attendant, 123, 159, 161

P

plantation
slave hospital, 16, 43, 48, 49, 64,
    68, 69, 70, 71, 72, 73, 74, 75,
    76, 78, 79, 114, 115, 116, 163
Southern, 16, 43, 48, 49, 64, 68,
    69, 70, 71, 72, 73, 74, 75, 76,
    78, 79, 114, 115, 116, 163
prisoner of war
British, 15, 32, 33, 154

R

research
modern medical, 98
revolutionary advancements
antiseptics, 134, 135, 176
hospitals, 15, 16, 7, 8, 10, 12, 13,
    14, 16, 17, 18, 19, 30, 40, 41,
    48, 55, 60, 64, 125, 126, 131,
    132, 133, 145, 148, 150, 151,
    155, 159, 160, 161, 165, 168,
    171, 172, 174, 175, 178, 181
nursing, 13, 1, 2, 9, 72, 73, 126,
    149, 158, 159, 160, 161, 162,
    167
organization, 12, 13
surgery, treatments, and
    specialization, 13, 62
rheumatic
arthritis, 29, 117, 189, 193

S

seasoning, 48, 51
slave
African, 12, 13, 16, 17, 22, 47, 48,
    49, 51, 52, 53, 55, 56, 59, 60,
    62, 64, 65, 66, 67, 68, 69, 70,
    71, 72, 73, 74, 75, 77, 78, 79,
    83, 84, 86, 88, 93, 96, 97, 98,
    99, 100, 101, 102, 103, 104,
    105, 107, 109, 110, 111, 112,
    114, 115, 116, 117, 118, 119,
    120, 121, 122, 123, 124, 129,
    163, 180, 183, 202, 218, 220

241